FURTHER ADVENTURES

OF THE

GREAT DETECTIVE

JOHN WILSON MURRAY

John Wilson Murray was born in Scotland on June 25, 1840. His father, a sea captain, soon moved the family to New York. Following the family tradition Murray went to sea, enlisting in the United States Navy in 1857.

As a sailor during the American Civil War, he had his first experience of the mystery and fascination of detective work, uncovering a plot to free 4,000 Confederate prisoners from an island prison in Lake Erie.

After the war he worked as a special agent for the U.S. Navy Department before joining the Police Force in Erie, Pennsylvania. He left Erie to become Head of Detectives of the Canadian Southern Railway and moved to Canada to establish his headquarters in St. Thomas, Ontario.

His success in the railway police brought Murray to the attention of Sir Oliver Mowat, then Attorney General of Ontario. In 1874 Murray became the Provincial Detective of Ontario and spent the rest of his life solving crimes committed in the province.

His death, in 1906, was front page news. The old Toronto Globe *included these words in its long obituary.*

"His fame was international, thousands of people knew him by sight, many hundreds prized the pleasure of his acquaintance. In his time he travelled through most every known country, and he frequently attained success in his objective when others had given up in despair, declaring the task beyond the bounds of human achievement."

FURTHER ADVENTURES

OF THE

GREAT DETECTIVE

INCIDENTS IN THE LIFE OF

John Wilson Murray

COLLINS

TORONTO

1980

ACKNOWLEDGEMENTS

Our thanks to Mr. A. Salam, Head, Social Sciences Department, Metropolitan Toronto Library for loaning us their copy of the original edition; and to William Heinemann Ltd., London, England for permission to reproduce the text of their original 1904 edition.

First published 1904 by William Heinemann Ltd.
London, England
This edition published 1980
by Collins Publishers
100 Lesmill Road, Don Mills, Ontario.

© 1980 by Wm. Collins Sons & Co. Canada Ltd.

Canadian Cataloguing in Publication Data

Murray, John Wilson, 1840-1906.
Further adventures of the great detective

Selections from the original work, published 1904
under title: Memoirs of a great detective.
Previous selections published Collins, 1977 under
title: Memoirs of a great Canadian detective.

ISBN 0-00-216816-2

1. Murray, John Wilson, 1840-1906.
2. Detectives—Ontario—Biography. I. Title.
II. Title: Memoirs of a great detective.
III. Title: Memoirs of a great Canadian detective.
HV7914.M87   363.2'5'0924   C80-094715-0

Printed in Canada

CONTENTS

1   KNAPP: A WEAZENED WONDER   9
2   THE FEMININE FIRM OF HALL AND CARROLL   16
3   THE EPISODE OF POKE SOLES   22
4   WITH THE HELP OF JESSIE McLEAN   25
5   WHEN RALPH FINDLAY LURCHED AND FELL   27
6   THE TINKLING HOUSE OF WELLINGTON
        SQUARE   36
7   APROPOS OF HUNKER CHISHOLM   40
8   THE MONAGHAN MURDER   44
9   THE FATAL ROBBERY OF THE DAINS   48
10   "AMER! AMER! AMER!"   61
11   McPHERSON'S TELLTALE TROUSERS   66
12   THE DISAPPEARING STORES   70
13   MARY ANN WEATHERUP, COQUETTE   77
14   THE CAPTURE OF LOCHINVAR SPROULE   81
15   BIG MAC OF SIMCOE, YOUNG SMITH, AND
        BILL NAY   87
16   THE NEW YEAR'S MURDER OF STILLWELL
        OF BAYHAM   93
17   THE WINTER ROAD TO MANITOULIN   96
18   THE LONG POINT MYSTERY   100
19   JOHN STONE, GENTLEMAN   107
20   BATES OF ALLANBURG'S FUNERAL PYRE   116
21   A SPREADER OF ARSENIC   121
22   FOR A MESS OF POTTAGE   125
23   "SHET-BLACK HERRES OF THE
        DING-DONG MUSTACHEES"   130

24 OLD JOHN KLIPPERT OF WATERLOO   139
25 TWO DISAPPEARANCES   145
26 THE HOLLOWED CHOCOLATE   151
27 THE FOOTMARK BY LANGFORD'S BED   154
28 THE LADY OF THE PIERCING BLACK EYES   160
29 AN ESCAPER OF GENIUS   165
30 PENNYFATHER OF THE BANK   172
31 THE GANGS OF PURTCH AND RUTLEDGE   176
32 THE KILLING OF JAMES AGNEW   181
33 OLIVE ADELE SEVENPIPER STERNAMAN   186
34 FOOLISH FRANK OSIER AND WISE SAM
        LINDSAY   191
35 EDDIE ELLIOTT, BOY MURDERER   195
36 DEMURE DATE PENDER OF EMSDALE   199
37 LEE CLUEY OF CATHAY   201
38 THE THREE DYNAMITARDS   204
39 THE TEMPORARY QUIRK MYSTERY   218
40 TWO CROOKS IN CLOVER   221

INTRODUCTION

In the 1870's and 1880's Canada was still a world where men and women faced a lifetime of back breaking effort to wrest a living from the land. The remoteness and loneliness of many of the pioneer settlements made the inhabitants perfect victims for crime.

Their physical isolation in the wilderness was compounded by the difficulty of transportation and communication, and the general lack of education. This was an era when people locked and barred their door at sundown and depended on their own guns as the first, and often the only, line of defense.

Most of the crime Murray saw was personal and brutal. In that largely unregulated age, what is now called whitecollar crime was either legal or, because of the local cash and barter economy, impossible. With travel beyond the reach of most settlers, criminals were usually found in the immediate area.

While far ahead of his time in the scientific investigation of crime, Murray's attitude toward the criminals his society produced was typical of the time. He believed that the criminal was a bad type, likely unrepentant and probably unsalvageable. Crime was genetic and ran in families, and criminals were the clear enemy of society. The detective's job, clear and simple, was to catch the criminals and prove their guilt so that the court could hand out a suitable punishment.

Despite all the crime he had seen, Murray believed that society had little to fear from criminals so long as the laws were strictly enforced. At the end of his long career, spent largely in the company of criminals and amongst the roughest elements of the Canadian wilderness, he thought the world a "grand place."

> I suppose I should take the view that this world is a wicked, dangerous place, infested with masked murderers or desperate workers in the darkness. But I hold no such opinion.
>
> This world is a grand place, life is a glorious thing. Crime increases, but not out of proportion to the increase in population of our countries and the whole world. Where men and women are, there will be found good and bad.

The first edition of the *Memoirs* of John Wilson Murray was published in London, England, in 1904. The editor, Mr. Victor Speer, inserted his own voice throughout the text, and it is probable that he had a large hand in turning Murray's memoirs into a coherent narrative.

It is Speer's presence, as a sort of Dr. Watson, recording the Great Detective's deeds, that is responsible for the repeated use of "Murray said" and "Murray did" throughout the text.

Readers interested in more of John Wilson Murray's true adventures will want to read *Memoirs of a Great Canadian Detective* (Collins, 1977) which contains the remaining material originally published in the one volume 1904 edition.

Michael Worek
Port Hope, 1980

1

KNAPP: A WEAZENED WONDER

A PLAGUE of sneak-thieving broke out in Erie in 1869, shortly after Murray became a detective. It grew to be epidemic. Furniture vanished out of houses. Clothing seemed to fall upon the backs of invisible wearers and saunter into Spookland. Ploughs disappeared from farmers' fields, as if they had started on the shortest route to China. Horses trotted off into nowhere. Entire shelves in stores were swept bare in a single night, and from one of them twenty dozen pairs of shoes seemed to walk out of sight at midday.

"'We had better order the people to anchor their houses, said Crowley to me," says Murray, in telling the story. "We watched all day and we watched all night for weeks, but the stealing went on just the same. Crowley said it must be giant rats, who had a den in the bowels of the earth and decided to furnish it from Erie. He said some one had told him that in India they had a plague, by which people wasted away and finally dried up. He concluded that the plague had spread from India to Erie, and had seized upon everything portable in and around the town. 'They're not stolen, they just waste away,' said Crowley. 'It's a case of now you see them, now you don't.' To clinch this, one of the men began to lose his hair. Crowley pointed to it and exclaimed: 'See, it's just wasting away.' I had a moustache that was not flourishing just then and I shaved it off. When I appeared for duty the next day Crowley gasped:

"'Great Scott, Murray! They didn't steal your moustache, did they?'

"Finally, a new democrat waggon disappeared. It belonged to James Tolwarthy, a grocer, who had left it in front of his store the day after he had paid $275 for it. The democrat

9

had gone, as completely as if a modern Elijah had impressed it for chariot service to the skies. Tolwarthy was angry. He kept his waggons usually in a hotel shed near his store. When he went there to look for his new democrat he found an old crackey waggon standing in its stead. It stood there for weeks, and every day we went to look at it, as if its tongue could tell us who left it there.

" We searched every stable and every vacant building in the town. Not a trace of Tolwarthy's democrat or of any other vanished property did we find. A little child can lead us, however, and I came across a boy who said he thought he had seen the man who left the waggon in Tolwarthy's shed. He described him as best he could. It was not much of a description, but a poor description is as good as a good photograph any day. I would rather have a fair description than a dozen photographs when it comes to going after a man I never saw. I took the lad's description and started out to visit every farmhouse on every road leading out of Erie. I nosed into all of them for a radius of several miles. I found no such man as the lad described, and no hay-mow hid any plunder either, for I climbed into all of them.

" At last I found a farmer who had seen a fellow drive by his house in a new democrat about the time Tolwarthy's waggon vanished and the description of the democrat tallied with that of Tolwarthy's democrat, while the description of the man proved him the same fellow seen by the lad.

" Crowley, Officer Snyder, and myself got a team and started to drive the road the stranger went with Tolwarthy's waggon. We stopped at every house along the way, but not a sign or trace of him could we find. For a dozen miles we made this farm-to-farm search. After fifteen miles or more we decided to put up the horses for a feed and rest. We turned off the main road, and in a secluded, out-of-the-way place, in a clearing with about twenty-five acres of pine woods around it, we saw a house. No one was in sight. We hailed, and presently a buxom, blooming woman, about twenty-five years old, seemed to pop out of nowhere and ask us if we wanted anything. Crowley asked for the man of the place, as he wanted to feed his horses. The woman whistled and out from a clump of bushes near the barn came a little, weazened old fellow, about fifty years old. He reminded me of a muskrat. The moment I laid eyes on him I recalled the description by the lad of the man who left the crackey waggon.

"We alighted and fed the horses. The old man eyed them keenly and looked at their teeth.

"' What's your name?' I asked him.

"' George Knapp,' he said.

"' Lived here long?'

"' Me and my wife been here about a year,' he answered.

"' Your wife?' I said.

"' Yep, ain't she a bloomer?' and the old man chuckled hideously as he leered at the young woman who was standing in the doorway of the house.

"He was keen as a scythe. I innocently asked him if he had seen any stranger driving past his house in a new democrat waggon.

"' Nope; no one ever drives past here,' said he. 'There ain't no past. The road stops here.'

"He parried us at every point. We searched his place, barn, house, and outbuildings and found nothing. Yet I was morally certain we had our man. As I sat in the shade by the barn I gazed idly at the stretch of cleared land running down to the creek. I noticed a place or two where the sod had been turned recently. It is the little things that point the way to big results. A signboard a foot long often tells you the road for the next forty miles.

"' Knapp,' I said, ' I am going fishing in that stream.'

"' All right,' said Knapp. 'Hope they bite.'

"' Lend me a spade,' I said.

"' What for?' said Knapp, with a sudden sharpening of his glance.

"' I want to dig some bait,' said I.

"Knapp hesitated, then brought a spade, and followed me as I set out for the stream. I halted at one of the spots where the sod had been turned.

11

" ' No good digging here,' said Knapp. 'Come on farther down.'

" ' Why ? ' said I.

" ' This has been dug,' said Knapp. ' It's worm-scarce right here.'

" Never mind,' said I. ' I only want a few, and it's easier digging.'

" The perspiration started on Knapp's weazened, wrinkled face. I never dally in my garden with my spade but I see a vision of Knapp dripping like an April shower.

" I drove in the spade. It struck something hard. I turned back the soil and there lay one of the wheels of Tolwarthy's democrat buried beneath a foot of earth. I looked at Knapp and he was grinning in a sickly sort of way. I called Crowley and Snyder and arrested Knapp. Then we led him down to the stream and sat down and informed the old man, on the edge of the water, that the wise thing for him to do was to confess the whole series of thefts. He looked at us and then at the water and then back at us. I think he understood. At any rate he stood up.

" ' Come on,' he said, and led the way to the house.

" The buxom woman met us at the door.

" ' Get the shingle,' said Knapp.

" Without a word she went indoors and returned with a broad shingle. It was covered with red dots, which Knapp explained were made with chicken blood. One big blotch was to show where the barn stood. The smaller dots spreading out beyond it showed where Knapp had buried the plunder.

" We began to dig. The first thing we struck was a coffin.

" ' You murderer ! ' said Snyder. ' Now we know why you used blood to dot the shingle.'

" We lifted the coffin carefully out of the grave. It was very heavy. We prized off the lid, expecting to see the mutilated body of one of Knapp's victims. Instead of a pallid face and glazed eyes we found dozens of boxes of shoes. Knapp chuckled.

" ' Coffins ain't only for corpuses,' he said.

12

"We unearthed samples of everything from a needle to an anchor, a shroud, a toilet set, a baby carriage, forty silk dresses, gold watches, seven ploughs, a harrow, surgical instruments, a churn, a log chain, a grandfather's clock, a set of grocer's scales, hats, overcoats, pipes, a barber's pole, even a policeman's shot gun, that cost one of the Erie policemen $80, and that Knapp had stolen from his house. One of us would dig for a while, then Knapp would dig, and if any one dug more than his share it was Knapp. We uncovered ten waggon loads of stuff, including Tolwarthy's democrat, which Knapp had buried piece by piece; even the bed or body of the waggon being interred behind a clump of bushes. It was the most wholesale thieving I had known. Old Knapp gloried in it, chuckling over each fresh discovery we made. The marvel of it all was how he had managed to steal the stuff. He swore to us that he had stolen it all single-handed, and I believe he did.

"We took Knapp and his wife to Erie, and locked them up. We hired a large vacant store in the Noble block in Erie, hauled in the plunder from Knapp's, and put it on exhibition for identification. It filled the place. Knapp had stolen enough to equip a department store.

"In burying his plunder he had boxed it up, preparatory to sending it away in the fall. He said frankly that he had been stealing for years. He explained that the way he did it was to drive into town in a waggon, pretending he was selling farm produce or garden vegetables, and seize opportunities in that way to familiarise himself with houses, and then sneak in later, and steal whatever he could carry away. No one seemed to know much about him, either who he was or whence he came. A year before he had settled in the secluded tract of timber, and had kept entirely to himself. He told me he had preyed on other places before he set out to steal everything portable in Erie, but never before had he been made to dig for two straight days uncovering his own plunder.

"Knapp was very angry over being compelled to work so steadily with a spade. He vowed he would get even. Sometime after he had been locked up in Erie, he called us in and informed us, in profound confidence, that he had buried $2,500 in gold out on his place, and if we would take him out there he would show us where it was. The story was plausible, and three of the fellows got a team, and drove out seventeen miles with Knapp to his place. They took three spades and a pick with them. Knapp began a lot of manœuvring, pacing off distances from house to barn, and from barn to tree, and from tree to stump. They followed him, and he tramped about for an hour, leading them through briars and swamps, and finally back toward the barn again.

" There is the place,' he announced.

" They began to dig as if their hope of eternal salvation depended on it. Knapp encouraged them to greater exertion, and told them he had buried the gold seven feet deep to have it secure. They toiled for hours, digging to a depth of eight feet, but finding nothing. One of them, who knew unbroken earth when he dug it, accused Knapp of tricking. The old man said he might have made a mistake in his measurements, and he led them off for another tramp through brush and wild wood, and ended up about ten feet from the hole they had dug just before.

" ' Ah, yes, I remember. This is the place,' said the old man. ' There is $2,500 in gold in two canvas bags.'

" They fell to again. It was a broiling hot day. They toiled until toward sundown, when the old man began to chuckle.

" ' That'll do,' he said. ' I'm even.'

" ' Even for what ? ' they asked.

" ' For the two days I had to dig,' said Knapp.

" ' And there's no gold here ? ' they demanded wrathfully.

" ' There's gold all right, but I cannot remember where it is,' said Knapp with a chuckle.

" They drove him back to Erie, and locked him up again. He was tried, convicted, and sentenced to sixteen years in the Alleghany Penitentiary. His wife was released. Knapp played insane, and beat the Penitentiary. He was transferred to the lunatic division, and, soon after, he sawed the bars, escaped, and never was caught. I saw him several

14

times in the Erie gaol before he was sent away.   He always was chuckling.

"' Murray,' he would say on each occasion, as I was leaving, 'remember you are leaving a man who never met a man who knew enough to be his partner.'

' What became of him no one knows.   He was a weazened wonder."

2

THE FEMININE FIRM OF HALL AND CARROLL

A COMPARATIVELY short time after Knapp was sent away thieving began again in Erie. It was not on quite the same wholesale basis, but what was lacking in quantity was present in quality, for the thieves made it a point to steal the finest silver ware and jewellery. Instead of sneak-thieving it was burglary. The marks of jemmies on doors and windows were sufficient to demonstrate this.

"Crowley thought at first that Knapp might have returned and changed his tactics," said Murray. "We drove out to Knapp's and made sure he was not there, although after his escape from the penitentiary no one could tell what had become of him. I was satisfied from the outset that Knapp had no hand in the thieving. Knapp prided himself on his cleverness as a sneak thief. Burglary would be a clumsy way of stealing, according to Knapp's ideas.

"After the second or third job it was apparent that no lone burglar was at work. There was a gang, for some of the jobs necessarily called for a watcher or lookout on the outside while a pal was inside a house. Silver ware, fine clothing, and jewellery began to disappear with a regularity that reminded us often of the day when Knapp was in his prime. Mr. Skinner's house was ransacked and a great quantity of silverware taken, and soon after the Skinner robbery the home of Mr. Bliss was plundered and a big haul of silver ware and jewellery was made.

"Crowley was worried. So were the rest of us. We put in about twenty hours a day, and I verily believe we scrutinised every man in and around Erie. We made every stranger account for himself. We gathered in all our regulars in the suspicious character line. We redoubled our patrol pre-cautions at night. It was of no avail. The burglaries went on just the same. One night a house in one end of the town would be robbed and the next night the burglars would do a job in the other end of the town. The only clue or trace of them that I could get was a peculiarity in the jemmy marks, showing a piece had been chipped or cut out of the jemmy. But to tell the truth we were at our wits' end and could make no headway. There were so many burglaries, yet we could not get on to them.

"Our last hang out at night was the Reed House. We would step in there regularly before going to bed. As we stood talking in the Reed House in the early morning hours or shortly after midnight, I noticed by the merest chance a woman slip quietly down the back stairs and out into the night. For three or four nights I observed her doing this. The clerk told me she was a scrubwoman, who worked late and lived outside the hotel. There was nothing suspicious about that. I asked the clerk where she lived. He said he did not know. It was a pleasant night and I felt like taking a walk, and just for amusement I decided to follow the old scrubwoman. She slipped down the back stairs as usual and went out. I trailed after her. We had not gone five blocks when I lost her. She seemed to have been swallowed up by some hole in the earth that vanished after devouring her. I laughed at the joke on me, unable to trail an old woman, and I went to bed.

"The next morning Crowley was glum. 'Another bur-glary last night,' he said, and named a house about four blocks from where I lost the old woman. I said nothing, but that night I was at the Reed House, waiting for my old scrubwoman. About one o'clock in the morning she appeared, a flitting figure on the back stairs, and darted out. I was after her in a jiffy. For about fifteen blocks I followed her. Then she suddenly turned a corner and when I came up she was gone. The next morning Crowley was mad as a hornet. 'Another burglary last night,' said he. I was a little hot myself. But that night I turned up at the Reed House, and at one o'clock out came my vanishing scrubwoman again and away she went, with me on her trail.

" I have shadowed many people in my life, but that old scrubwoman was one of the most artful dodgers I ever knew. I followed her from one o'clock until after four o'clock in the morning, up streets and down streets, through alleys, across lots, around buildings, and then across lots again. But I stuck to her and there was no corner she turned that I was not close up to spot her if she dodged. Soon after we started a cat suddenly mewed and startled her mightily. Along about dawn she headed away to the outskirts of the town and stopping in front of a double house tossed a pebble up against a window and a moment later went in. I sat down some distance away and thought it all over. I was puzzled. Women burglars were something unknown in Erie or anywhere else, just then. Yet to think that an old woman after scrubbing for hours in an hotel would go out for a stroll and prowl around all night for her health was out of the question. I waited until broad daylight and when she did not come out I went to headquarters.

" ' Another one last night, Murray,' said Crowley.

" Then it could not have been my old scrubwoman, for I had her in sight every minute. However, I determined to pay her a visit. I took Jake Sandusky of the police force, who now is the Pennsylvania Railway detective, with head-quarters at Erie, and went out to the house. On one side of the double house lived Mrs. O'Brien, a respectable woman. She knew nothing of the occupants of the other side of the house, beyond the fact that they were women and had lived there less than a year.

" I knocked at the door. There was no answer. I banged again, loud and long. I heard a scurry of feet inside and finally the door opened. A big, fine-looking girl, about twenty-three years old, stood in the doorway. I walked right in.

" ' What is your name ? ' I asked her.

" ' Mary Ann Hall,' said she.

" ' Do you live alone ? ' said I.

" ' I live with my mother,' said Mary Ann.

18

"'Call your mother,' I said.

"Mary Ann opened wide her mouth and let out a bawl like a donkey's bray.

"'Ma-a-a-aw!' she bellowed.

"Out from the adjoining room pranced my old scrubwoman as sprightly and spry as any being of sixty years I ever saw.

"'What's your name?' I asked.

"'Mrs. Julia Hall,' said my old scrubwoman, and if ever there is a gallery for the portraits of sixty-year old coquettes I will contribute the picture of Julia Hall.

"'Who else lives here?' I asked.

"The answer was the opening of Mary Ann's mouth in another prolonged bellow.

"'Ma-a-ag-gie!' she shouted.

"Out from the adjoining room trotted a second old woman, a little bit of a body about fifty years old, with a face like an eagle's. She had a loose ringlet that flipped around her cheek, and she constantly blew at it out of the side of her mouth to fleck it back to her ear.

"'Ladies,' said I, 'sit down.'

"To my astonishment all three promptly sat on the floor I observed that the chief articles of furniture in the room were a cook stove, a rough kitchen table, and one dilapidated rocking chair.

"'Mrs. Julia Hall,' I say, and I can see her coy leer as she sat on the floor, 'you were out all night, last night.'

"'I always am,' she said.

"'Yes, Julia cannot sleep in the dark,' spoke up the eagle-faced woman, who hastened to add apologetically, 'I am Mrs. Maggie Carroll, her friend.'

"'I never sleep in the night,' said Mrs. Hall. 'I work or walk all night, and when daylight comes I sleep.'

"'It's an affliction,' said Mrs. Carroll. 'She had the fever when she was a child.'

"I talked on with these three strange creatures squatted on the floor. They puzzled me. I mentioned the burglaries to them. They knew nothing of them, they said. Mrs. Carroll was particularly vehement in protestations of ignorance. I crossed over and sat down in the dilapidated rocker beside

19

the range. There was a kettle on the stove, but no fire. Suddenly the chair collapsed with a crash. Over I went with my heels in the air. One of my feet struck the kettle and it fell to the floor and the lid rolled off. The three women had laughed uproariously when the chair broke down ; Mary Ann haw-hawing, Mrs. Hall tittering, and Mrs. Carroll cackling. But when the kettle fell and its top rolled off there was sudden silence. I looked at the three women and then at the chair and then I saw the kettle. Its top was towards me and inside I observed what I thought was a stove lifter. I reached for it and drew it out. It was a jemmy ! Moreover, it was a nicked jemmy !

"I stood up and eyed the three women. Mrs. Carroll feigned weeping, but Mrs. Hall tittered and made saucer eyes, as if bent on conquest, even on the penitentiary's verge.

"'Mary Ann,' I said, ' you might save me the trouble of searching the house by hauling out the plunder.'

"At this Mrs. Hall struck Mary Ann a resounding whack on the head and bade her : 'Squat where you be, you hussy ! '

"I searched the house. I found silverware, jewelry, linen, fine clothes in amazing quantities. The Skinner silverware, the Bliss silverware, the plunder from many houses, all was recovered. I found also a complete set of pass-keys and a house-breaking kit of burglar's tools.

"We arrested the three women. All three were tried. Two, Mrs. Julia Hall and Mrs. Maggie Carroll, were sent to Alleghany for four years, and Mary Ann was let off. While in gaol Mary Ann gave birth to a bouncing baby. I asked Mrs. Hall about her tramp through the night when I was following her. She laughed in a flirtatious way that was ludicrous. From Mrs. Carroll I learned that she and Mrs. Carroll were to have done another job that night, and Mrs. Hall was to meet Mrs. Carroll at two o'clock in the morning. But Mrs. Carroll had spied me trailing Mrs. Hall, and had mewed suddenly like a cat, a signal to Mrs. Hall that she was being followed. That was the cat's cry that had startled Mrs. Hall, and caused her to prowl around all night and not go home till morning.

" They were the only pair of professional women burglars working alone that I ever met red-handed. They had been caught first in Ireland and were sent to Australia, when they got into trouble again and jumped to the United States. Mrs. Julia Hall was the genius of the two. I often thought that she was foolish to use a nicked jemmy. Her cracked smile would have broken into almost anything."

3

THE EPISODE OF POKE SOLES

POKE SOLES was a " shover of the queer." An episode of
his life occurred at Erie, following the capture of the women
burglars, which reveals now for the first time the story of
Tom Hale, a counterfeiter, who subsequently was a side-
member of the United States Secret Service. Poke's duties
as a shover of the queer were to pass counterfeit money.

" In the winter of 1869 and 1870 some $20 bills that were
queer, appeared in Erie," says Murray. " It was some time
after the women burglars had been tried and sentenced.
Fred Landers kept a restaurant in Erie, and one day I happened to drop in, and he told me of a fellow who had been in
and ordered a light lunch and paid for it with a $20 bill, and
who bought a drink as he went out and offered a second $20 bill
to the bar-tender, who said he could not change it. I looked
at the banknote Landers had taken. It was a clever one,
but it was queer. My experience with counterfeiters in
the special service of the United States was of instant value
Landers described the man. I spotted him at the railroad
station and got him, but did not find any of the stuff or
counterfeit money on him. He simply was a shover, one who
passed the money, and he received only a couple of $20
bills at a time.

" Few classes of crime are organised so scientifically as
counterfeiting. The man who makes the plates never does
business with the men who pass the money. The plate-maker
is an engraver who usually gets a lump sum for his work.
Those who print the money are the manufacturers and they
sell the queer in wholesale quantities to dealers, who sell
to retail dealers, who have their shovers out passing the
money. The man I got was a shover. I locked him up and
in searching him I found the name ' Tom Hale, New York.'

I reported to Crowley and sent a telegram addressed to Hale and reading:

"'Come on. I am sick. Stopping at Morton House. Room 84.'

"I made all arrangements with the hotel clerk to get track of any one who called and asked for the man in room 84. No one came. I kept the shover, whose name was Soles, locked up in gaol. Landers and the bar-tender had identified him. A week passed. It was in the winter of 1870 and the trains were blockaded and it snowed and blew and delayed all traffic. On the ninth day a nice looking man walked into the Morton House. It was bitter cold and yet he had no overcoat. He asked for Mr. Soles in room 84. I was in the hotel at the time; the clerk tipped me and I walked over and collared the stranger. I took him down and searched him and locked him up. He had several hundred dollars of good money on him, but no counterfeit money. I intended to hold him while I hunted for his baggage, for at least a man dressed as he was, would have an overcoat somewhere near.

"The next morning Officer Snyder and I went to the railroad station and began,¹ from there, a systematic search for trace of the stranger's overcoat. In the morning we were in the habit of stepping into John Anthony's German saloon for a mug of beer. On that morning Anthony said: 'A funny thing happened yesterday. A nice looking fellow came in and washed his hands and went away leaving his overcoat.'

"'Let me see it, John,' said I.

"Anthony produced the coat. In the first pocket in which I thrust my hand I found a roll of something wrapped in a handkerchief. I drew it out and found $1000 in counterfeit $20 and $100 bills, with coupons attached to the ends. They were such excellent counterfeits that later I passed one at a bank as a joke and then told them of it. I took the coat to the lockup.

"'Hello, Hale; here's your coat,' I said.

"'All right. Thank you,' said the stranger, who was Tom Hale.

"I said: 'That's your coat, Tom?'

"'Oh, yes,' said he.

23

"Then I hauled out the counterfeit money from the pocket. He then said it was not his coat. I made him put the coat on and it fitted him perfectly. Then John Anthony identified him as the stranger who had left the coat in his saloon.

"Soles was held for passing counterfeit money. He pleaded guilty and was sent to Alleghany for five years. The United States authorities took Hale to Pittsburg, then to New York, and then to Washington. He promised to do everything for the Secret Service Department. He was going to give away the whole counterfeiting business.

"Wood, then chief of the Secret Service, appointed him to the United States Secret Service and sent him to New York. Hale never gave any one away, but a few shovers and small Italians. In the meantime, Wood left the Service. Colonel Whiteley became chief. He sent for Hale and told him he was doing nothing. Hale practically told Colonel Whiteley to go to hell, which showed Hale was not so wise as some people seemed to think he was.

"Finally Hale was arrested and taken back to Pittsburg and tried. Butcher Swope was the United States prosecuting attorney. Hale was convicted and sentenced to fourteen years in the penitentiary. It was proved where he stood in with thieves. Butcher Swope was a cracking good prosecuting attorney, and a hard man after these crooked fellows.

"The last time I saw Tom Hale was about 1884. He was keeping a dime lodging house on the Bowery in New York at that time. He fared far worse in his sentence than did Poke Soles who stood up like a man when he was caught and did his time. I understand Hale never set foot in Erie again and vowed he never would. The most disappointed man was John Anthony, when the owner of the overcoat was found and the $1,000 turned out to be queer."

4

WITH THE HELP OF JESSIE McLEAN

On a bright, sunshiny day in 1874 Murray walked out of General-Superintendent Finney's office in the Canada Southern Station at St. Thomas. He had just returned from Cleveland, and had made a report on the arrest of a thief, who at one time had been bothersome to the company. As he strolled down the platform he saw a group of trainmen laughing and chatting and sunning themselves. They were talking of fires.

"Sparks from Canada Southern locomotives seemed to become contagious, and various buildings along the line began to shoot sparks and to go up in smoke," says Murray. "It grew to be bothersome, and the insurance companies became considerably wrought up. The complaints, of course, came to me.

"At that time one of the features of life in St. Thomas was Jessie McLean. Jessie was as bonnie a Scotch lass as a man could meet in twenty counties. She was good-looking, with peachy cheeks and sunny hair and merry eyes. But, above all, Jessie weighed 250 pounds. She was the biggest girl in St. Thomas. Some of the fellows used to joke at Jessie, but I always treated her with courtesy, and I remember the days when I used to walk a quarter of a mile just to see Jessie McLean on her way to church. It was not a case of love, but simply a desire to see a 250-pound girl go by. Every man, as he looks back through the years into the little town where he lived long ago, can recall certain sights and scenes that stand out vividly in the vision of his memory. 'Twas so with Jessie McLean. I can close my eyes and see her still, tripping churchward, 250 pounds of graceful femininity.

"But back to the burnings. The climax of the fires

came when the Dufferin House, in St. Thomas, burned. The Dufferin House was named after Lord Dufferin, then Governor-General of Canada. It was a large wooden building with sixty or more rooms, and stood on Talbert Street, near what is now the Michigan Central Station. Johnnie Hanley was the proprietor. He had $9,000 of mortgages on the house. The hotel was not paying, and Johnnie could not pay the mortgages.

"One quiet Sunday evening in October the Dufferin House was burned. No lives were lost. The insurance people were certain the fire was incendiary in its origin. Mr. Westmacott, the insurance representative from Toronto, came to me ; and I also heard the talk that engine sparks caused the fire. I took charge of the case. I began a search for evidence. It was a difficult task. The evidence was not connected in its chain of circumstances. Finally, I found the pastor of the Baptist Church could strengthen my cause ; but I still lacked the desired clinching testimony. Where was I to get it?

"The answer came in Jessie McLean. The 250-pound Scotch girl told me she had seen Johnnie Hanley as he came hurriedly off the back steps just before the fire. It completed the case, and, thanks to Jessie McLean, who had been on her way to church when she saw him, Johnnie Hanley was convicted and sentenced to seven years' imprisonment.

"Hanley had a son-in-law, Bill Cronin, who kept the Detroit House ; and subsequently it was burned. Assisted by Chief-of-Police James Fewings, who also aided me in the Hanley case, I convicted Cronin of setting the house on fire, and he also was sent to prison for seven years. After Cronin had followed Hanley to prison, the sparks of the Canada Southern engines seemed to become harmless ; for there were no more mysterious fires, and the insurance companies breathed easy, and Jessie McLean continued on her innocent, 250-pound way, and finally married a bouncing railroad conductor."

5

WHEN RALPH FINDLAY LURCHED AND FELL

IN the pale moonlight of a warm night, in September 1875, a door opened softly in the big farmhouse of Ralph Findlay, in the township of Sombra, county of Lambton, about a hundred and fifty miles west from Toronto, and a man stepped out. He was clad in nightshirt and trousers. In his hand he carried a lantern, that cast a circle of fitful light about him as he walked. He crossed swiftly from the house to the barn· There were noises in the barn. The horses were neighing and stamping. The figure with the lantern paused and listened, then hastened to the nearest door. The noises ceased as he approached. He stepped forward and opened the door. A shot rang out in the night. He choked, swayed, and fell forward on the floor, the lantern in his hand. So he lay.

The terrified squealing of the horses died away. Their stamping ceased. The minutes passed. A figure crept cautiously out of the barn, peering into the face of the man prone on the floor, and vanished in the night. The swish of his feet could be heard as he sneaked along in the shadow of the fence beyond the barn and near the house. Then all was still. No sound came from house or barn. The lantern in the stiffening hand had gone out. So had the life.

The door of the house opened cautiously a second time. A woman stood in the doorway. She held a light above her head and suddenly shouted: "Get up! Get up!" Lights popped out in the house. The woman and three men ran out of the house and across to the barn. They went straight to the nearest door. They peered in. The light of their lamps fell upon the lifeless figure on the floor.

"Oh, my God! The horses have kicked him to death! Go for my father!" shrieked the woman. One of the three men ran to the horses, bridled one of them, leaped upon him and went galloping through the night to the home of Farmer Rankin, nine miles away, to tell him that his daughter's husband had been kicked to death by the horses. The other men beside the body in the barn knelt and looked at the dead man, then crossed to the horses and found them in their stalls, but with their halters slipped. The woman ran screaming back to the house and to her two little children. The two men hastened for some of the neighbours. They came in the night and bore the body into the house. The Rankins, father and sons, came galloping with doctors before the dawn. But Ralph Findlay was beyond all need of doctors.

They started a coroner's inquest at once. Mrs. Findlay told how she was in bed with her husband, and they heard a noise in the barn. He got up, slipped on his trousers, and went out. He stayed so long that she became alarmed, arose, went to the door, heard nothing, and then roused the inmates of the house and ran to the barn, where they found him dead on the barn floor.

William Smith, the hired man, who rode away to notify the Rankins, told of being awakened by Mrs. Findlay's cries and going out to the barn and finding Findlay dead. The other hired men, Buchanan and Reed, told of being awakened and rushing out and finding the dead man. They were under the impression that horse thieves had sneaked into the barn to steal the horses, that Findlay had caught them in the act, and they had shot him and escaped. The Department of Justice at Toronto was notified by telegraph. Murray was near St. Thomas on another case. The Department telegraphed to him to go immediately.

" I arrived there on the day of the funeral," says Murray. " I never had seen such a crowd of farmers as had gathered there. I was a stranger to them all. Findlay was a highly esteemed, educated man. He had been a professor and had taught in various schools, and was considered one of the best mathematicians in the province. I learned from neighbours, who were at the place for the funeral, that several years before he had bought the farm of two hundred and fifty or more acres, stocked it well, and shortly before moving on to it he married Sarah Rankin, daughter of a big farmer in the adjoining township of Dover. She was a rosy, good-looking, stout woman of about twenty-seven when her husband was killed. He was a man of gentlemanly appearance and about thirty-eight years old. He had three hired men, Smith, Buchanan, and Reed, and also a hired girl. There were two children, a little boy and girl. The hired man Smith had gone away once and spent some months in the lumber woods of Michigan, but returned and resumed his work with Findlay.

"All was confusion and excitement around the place. Farmers were talking, and women were gathered in groups, some weeping, others full of anger or fear. I saw the hired girl out near the well and quietly learned what she knew. Smith, the hired man, had been to Wallaceburg, five miles away, on the evening of the murder, but had returned in good time and retired with the hired man Reed. The hired girl went to bed as usual, and was awakened by Mrs. Findlay's crying: 'Get up! Get up!' I next talked with Reed, a young fellow about nineteen years old. He said he and Smith slept together, that they went to bed as usual, that he slept soundly until he heard Mrs. Findlay shouting: 'Get up! Get up!' Reed jumped out of bed at once, he said, while Smith still was sleeping. He shook Smith, who was hard to waken, and they went downstairs and out to the barn. Buchanan, the hired man, told me his story too, similar to the others.

"I had not seen Mrs. Findlay or Smith. In fact, wherever I went I was followed by a throng of people, who dogged my footsteps and crowded forward when I stopped. Two of Findlay's brothers were there. One of them was a Customs officer at Port Stanley, and the other, John Findlay, was a merchant also at Port Stanley. John Findlay was in a frenzy of excitement. He went about exclaiming that his brother was murdered, and beseeching me to find the murderer.

"I drew back from the throng of country folk and looked them over. My eye lighted on the keen, intelligent face of an old fellow, and I walked over and called him aside. He said his name was McLean, and he lived about a mile away, his house being in plain view. We chatted, and suddenly the old fellow said :

"'This summer I was out looking for my cattle beyond the woods, and I stopped here for a drink of water. There was no cup at the pump. I walked into the kitchen and Smith and ·Mrs. Findlay were on the floor. She jumped up and said Smith was taking a thorn out of her foot.'

" While we were talking McLean nodded towards the outskirts of the crowd and said : 'You see that fellow in the blue shirt ? That's the hired man, William Smith.' I looked and saw a hangdog sort of fellow standing apart from the others. The minister had not arrived, so I sat quietly watching Smith, who chewed a piece of grass and paced slowly to and fro. The minister came and the crowd rushed around him, John Findlay shouting for justice. I walked through the house and out of the back door. I saw a stout woman back of the house, moaning and wringing her hands.

"' Oh, my God ! Oh, my God ! ' she was crying, swaying to and fro as she cried.

"' Are you Mrs. Findlay ? ' I asked.

"' Yes, yes. Oh, my God ! Oh, my God ! ' she cried.

"' Come here. I want you," I said roughly.

"' Oh ! ' she gasped.

" I led her well away from the house and the crowd, to a quiet corner where an old log lay. She sat down on the end of the log. I stood up. I looked at her fully five minutes without speaking or moving. She rocked to and fro, moaning and crying bitterly at first, and all the time exclaiming : 'Oh, my God ! Oh, my God ! ' But as the silence lengthened, I noticed her look at me through her fingers as she held her hands to her face. When she looked she ceased crying, but immediately would resume her lamentations and moans of ' Oh, my God ! Oh, my God ! '

"' You might well say : " Oh, my God ! " ' I exclaimed suddenly.

"' Oh, my God ! Oh, my God ! ' she answered, rocking violently.

" I bent over her with my face close to hers. 'Are you not afraid to mention the name of God, you murderer ? I do not sympathise with you, but I do sympathise with your two little children. Their father murdered, and their mother hanged!'

"'Oh, my God!' she moaned and shuddered.

"'Don't you dare say that,' I thundered. 'Speak some other name but not the name of God.'

"Suddenly Smith came into sight near the house.

"'Look at that villain!' I said to her, and she raised her head and looked toward the house and saw Smith.

"'Oh, my God!' she shrieked.

"'I told you before not to call your God to witness," I said, my mouth close to her ear. 'You know what your God knows of this!'

"'Oh, oh, oh!' she gasped and put up her hands as if to shut away a hateful sight.

"She began to pant like a hound that is exhausted. She gasped and clutched at the empty air. She rocked and swayed and beat her clenched hands together and struck herself upon the forehead, temples, and bosom. I waited. The vision of the crime was before her, the clutch of the sense of guilt was choking her. She writhed in mental and moral agony. She shut her eyes and turned away her head, but turn where she would, the crime confronted her.

"'Out with it!' I said. 'Tell me the truth. I want nothing but the truth.'

"She looked up and her eyes were like those of an ox in whose throat the butcher's knife has been buried.

"'Oh!' she husked, in a hoarse whisper. 'Will you hang me?'

"'I am not in a position to say what will become of you, but I do pity your children,' I answered.

"With a gulp she lurched back, clutched at the log, sat up and, dry-eyed and sobless, told me the story of the crime. She blamed Smith at the outset. She said he did it and had caused all the trouble. When he went to Michigan to the lumber camps it was because her husband had discharged him. While in Michigan, Smith had corresponded with her, and had brought to her a bottle of strychnine, with which she was to poison her husband. She had failed to do it, but

31

when Smith returned she persuaded her husband, much against his will, to hire Smith again. On the evening of the murder she gave Smith $1 to go to Wallaceburg, five miles away, to buy a bottle of brandy to give him courage. He bought the brandy and came back and went to bed as usual, sleeping on the outside of the bed he shared with young Reed. He sneaked out when he thought all were asleep, went to the barn, untied the horses, and began to slash them so that they would make a noise. Mrs. Findlay woke her husband and told him he'd better go out to the barn. He went, and Smith shot him as he entered. No one but Mrs. Findlay heard the shot. She arose when she heard it, and let Smith into the house. 'I finished him,' said Smith, as he entered. 'Good boy,' she said, and closed the door. Smith had another drink and went upstairs to bed, and after all was still she opened the door and began to cry: 'Get up! get up!'

"As she sat on the log she told me the story. I immediately got John Findlay, the brother, and old man McLean I gave Findlay a book and pencil and she told the story again, while he wrote it down.

"'Go back to the house and the crowd,' I said to her, when she finished. 'Don't open your mouth or say a word to that murderer. I am not going to arrest him now.'

"She started back, tearless and no longer moaning.

"'Begin to sob,' I told her, and straightway she resumed her moaning and crying, with mutterings of 'Oh, my God! Oh, my God!'

"The minister began the service. The hearse arrived. The coffin was carried out. The people entered their waggons. The procession was about to start. I was watching Smith. I saw him hang back and I sent old man McLean to him.

"'Smith, ain't you going to the funeral?' asked McLean.

"'No,' said Smith. 'Too much to do.'

"'Go on and get your coat or people will say you did it,' said McLean.

"Smith got into a waggon and drove to the cemetery. He was placed well up toward the grave. They lowered the coffin. Some clods fell on it with a rattle and a thud. Smith turned his back. I stood right behind him. As he turned I said, right in his ear : ' Go and take your last look at the man you murdered.'

" He started as if he had been knifed.

" ' I ain't murdered no one,' he said, pale as a candle.

" ' Go, look at that coffin, going down into the grave,' I said.

" He would not look. It seemed as if he could not look. I arrested him, and, calling the constable, had him taken away quietly and locked up. It did not disturb the burial.

" Then came the battle. I foresaw the tremendous elements of influence that would rally to avert a conviction. I reopened the inquest, put Mrs. Findlay on the stand and she told her story. She and Smith were committed to Sarnia gaol. I searched the house and found the strychnine in the bottle. I went to Michigan and made a tour of the drug stores, and in St. Louis, Michigan, I found the druggist who sold the bottle of poison to Smith. I proved by young Reed that the gun used to shoot Findlay was kept in the barn, and Reed had seen Smith reload it a few days before the murder. While Mrs. Findlay was telling her story on the stand, Smith burst out : ' Oh, you villain, you will hang both of us.' Her answer was characteristic : ' Oh, my God ! '

" While Mrs. Findlay and Smith were in gaol awaiting the trial, she corresponded with Smith, writing him notes and lowering them from her cell window to his cell window, by means of a thread made by unravelling her stocking. The gaoler finally got the correspondence, and it was turned over to the sheriff ; but when called for in court it was not to be found. The failure to produce it caused a great deal of talk.

" Judge Moss presided at the trial. He is dead now and this case came in his first year on the bench. The Crown was represented by the present Judge MacMahon, a descendant of the distinguished French MacMahons. Smith was defended by a very able lawyer, David Glass, of London, now dead. Smith belonged to a prominent order, of which no member ever was hung in that county. At the assizes, in October 1875, Smith was tried and convicted of murder.

In Canada there are no verdicts of degrees of murder. A prisoner is guilty of murder or manslaughter, or is acquitted, or the jury disagrees. When a prisoner is convicted of murder, the judge has no alternative but to sentence him to be hanged. For manslaughter the sentence may be for life or for any less term down to three months. At the trial of Smith, Mrs. Findlay went on the stand and swore to her story.

" Mr. Glass took an objection to the legality of the evidence. It was carried to the Court of Appeal of the Province, then to the Supreme Court of Canada, and finally to the Privy Council in England. It was a precedent case. The Privy Council sustained the rulings of the trial judge, that Mrs. Findlay's evidence was admissible under the circumstances. It was over a year after Smith's conviction, when the Privy Council passed on the case. Smith was sentenced to be hanged. Through the influence of his counsel, who was a very prominent party man at that time, his sentence was commuted to imprisonment for life. He died in the Penitentiary after serving fifteen years, or more. Mrs. Findlay was in gaol for a couple of years, or more, and finally was released without trial, and went back to her people. Smith was about thirty-two years old, and vastly unlike the man he murdered, either in appearance or education.

" It was a case in which the countryside at first was united on the theory of horse thieves. To me the theory was worthless, for the horse thieves would not have unhaltered four horses and turned them loose in a barn, but would have haltered them and led them quietly out. It was a case where, the general history of all concerned, prior to the crime, supplied the possibility of an adequate motive in the form of a desire to be rid of Findlay. The woman's grief was sham. McLean's thirst in the summer which caused him to walk unannounced into the kitchen of the Findlay house, led to the clue that caused me, upon seeing how unreal was the woman's sorrow, to crowd her for a confession. Her imagination pictured to her the crime when she strove in vain to shut it out. Imagination is the key that has unlocked the secret of many a crime. Imagination conjures up all the potent fears that the guilty dread. It causes many crimes, but it also betrays many a criminal."

6

THE TINKLING HOUSE OF WELLINGTON SQUARE

NEAR the main road leading through Wellington Square, a little place twenty-five miles west of Toronto and a convenient drive from Hamilton, stood the farmhouse of an old man named Pettit. Neighbours who passed in the night averred that at unusual hours a light shone and there was a tinkling sound such as they could not account for. They used to creep close and listen. They could hear the tinklety-tink, tinklety-tink, like the muffled tapping of a tiny bell, yet different from a bell's clear voice.

The old man kept to himself. He had a son who lived with him, and they were uncommunicative about their affairs. They were industrious and thrifty. Their crops were good, their cattle were fat, their expenses were small. Finally a neighbour, bolder than the others, was passing the house one night and hearing the faint, insistent tinklety-tink, he crept close, and finally climbed a tree and peered into the window. The sight made him gasp. A candle stood on the table. Beside the candle was a box as big as a washboiler. Old man Pettit stood by the box. His face was beaming, his eyes were bright. On the table was a heap of gold, not a little heap, but a big pile, with gold coins scattered all over the table. They shone and glittered in the candle-light. The old man would thrust his hands into the pile, seize the gold coins until he could hold no more, raise his hands and then drop the coins in golden streams down on to the pile again. As they struck the yellow pyramid they clinked and tinkled musically. At the sound of the gold the old man would laugh like a little child. His gold was the joy of his life.

After delving in this treasure to his heart's content, the old man gathered the gold pieces carefully into piles and placed them in the box. Then he blew out the candle and was lost in the darkness.

The neighbour climbed down out of the tree. He had solved the mystery of the tinkling house. He was an honest man and said nothing. But gradually others came to know that Pettit distrusted banks, and was said to keep a large sum of money in his house or buried on his farm.

"This talk spread until, in the country round about, Pettit was regarded as a man living in a treasure house," says Murray. "In the spring of 1875, before I became connected with the Government, Pettit went to Hamilton with a lot of fat cattle, and sold them for a good price. He was spotted ; and when he did not put his money in a bank, the spotters made sure where he lived and let him go unmolested. A few nights later a waggon drove up to a dark spot near the Pettit house. Four masked men alighted. They went on foot to the Pettit house and knocked upon the door. The old man answered the knock, and when he opened the door they knocked him down, while his son ran out of the house and across fields, and hid in the woods a mile away. They ransacked the house, discovered the box, and emptied out the gold. There was $10,500 in gold. Despite the old man's pleadings they took the gold and went away.

"The old man raised a great hubbub and four men were arrested in Hamilton, taken before a police magistrate and promptly acquitted. They were very highly connected and a large number of the leading lawyers appeared for them. The affair ran along until November 1875. Politics had become mixed up in it, some alleging that the reason the men were not prosecuted was, that their friends had a large amount of political influence. No doubt they had. Finally a demand was made on the Department of Justice to have the matter investigated. I had become connected with the Department in July, and when the complaint came in I was instructed to take the matter up. I knew at the outset that, owing to certain matters, I could not look for much assistance in Hamilton. Every detective must expect such conditions occasionally to confront him. So must men in other businesses. Friendships are friendships, and business is business, and there may be times when the ties of one are as strong as the rules of the other.

"I set out to learn what became of the gold. I learned that some of it had appeared in Brantford the morning after the robbery, so it was probable the robbers had gone to Brantford and divided it. My suspicions were correct. They had divided the booty in Brantford and had bought wine there. I learned also that they had hired the waggon in Hamilton. I got track of one of the four men in the United States. He was a professional burglar and thief. He has reformed since, and now is living in Buffalo, and I would be quite as ready to trust him as a lot of other people who lay strenuous claim to respectability. I had known him of old, and had landed him for seven years once. That was long before he reformed. He had his share in the Pettit gold, for he had done his part in the Pettit robbery.

"I learned, by tracing the gold in various places where it was spent, that the chief figure in the robbery was Charles Mills, of Hamilton. He was highly connected with leading people and had gone to Texas. He was far from being a poor man, having $50,000 or so, and, in addition, a rich old aunt, who was expected to leave him a fortune. I planned various ways to get him back into Canada, but none worked. Finally, I got track of a girl in Hamilton, named Lil White, of whom he was very fond. I had scoured the country for miles around in hunt of gold that had been spent and in search of information about Mills. I heard of the White girl through an acquaintance of Mills, and through Lil White I put up a job on Mills, and lured him back to Canada. I caught him in Hamilton on Sunday night, December 12th, 1875. I convicted him, too. Among the witnesses was Detective Patrick Mack of Buffalo, and I traced where they spent some of the gold there.

"The case, of course, attracted considerable attention, because of the influence of the friends of some of those involved. The late B. B. Osler, then County Crown Attorney in Hamilton, prosecuted. The prisoners were defended ably by William Laidlaw, K.C., of Hamilton, now of Toronto, and by the present Judge Robertson. Mills was convicted of robbery on January 14th, 1876, at Milton, and was sentenced to five years' imprisonment. Subsequently he was pardoned through the efforts of political friends. Politics cut no figure in the conviction, but it did in the pardon. Mills demanded a speedy trial instead of a trial by jury, and he was tried by the county judge without a jury. In Canada you can waive the right of a jury trial and demand what is termed a speedy trial. The Act was just passed at that time.

"After the trial and sentence, old man Pettit began an action against the Mills estate for the $10,500 of his gold that had been stolen. He got a judgment, and collected all the money with interest. Then he began an action against his own lawyer for overcharging, and he beat him, too.

"Pettit was a man of deep-set characteristics. I remember that, when I set to work on the case for him, I went to his house at Wellington Square, and went over the ground. From there I desired to go to Milton, nine miles away.

" ' I will drive you over,' said old man Pettit.

" ' Thank you,' said I.

" He hitched up a horse and drove me the nine miles to Milton. When we arrived at Milton I alighted, thanking him, and bade him good-day.

" ' Just a minute,' said he. ' I'd like $1·75, please.'

" ' What for ? ' said I.

" ' For driving you over,' said he.

" ' But I am working on your case,' said I.

" ' I know that,' said he, ' so I used my son's rig and the bill is $1·75.'

" I paid it. If he had made it $2 he could have put it into gold."

7

APROPOS OF HUNKER CHISHOLM

When Murray arrived in Toronto his attention was called to a series of horse-stealings occurring in several adjoining counties. None but the finest horses disappeared.

"I went to investigate," says Murray, "and I met one of the most picturesque old crooks I ever became acquainted with. His name was Chisholm, George Chisholm, called by some of his friends, Hunker. He was an inveterate horse thief. He simply could not help it. In the many years I knew him he never stole anything else, but out of sixty years of life he spent about forty years in prison, all for stealing horses.

"Chisholm stole horses to order. Sometimes he would read the papers for advertisements of men who wanted to buy horses. He would cut out the description of a horse, go around the country hunting for an animal to match the description, and when he found such a horse he would steal it and go and sell it to the man who advertised. Sometimes he would spot or locate a fine horse, and would go and look him over carefully. Then he would go to some other county and hunt for a purchaser. He would describe the horse exactly as he was, and if the prospective purchaser seemed pleased and told him to bring the horse around, Chisholm would disappear, steal the horse, and in a few days reappear and sell him. He never stole anything else. He never was a born burglar except for horses. He never robbed a house. He simply was a horse thief. From time to time he would get caught and sent down to a stiff term, but at its expiration he would bob up serenely, and horses would begin to disappear again.

"When I was investigating the horse thefts I recalled that

a tailor named Spellman had been arrested in the town of Vienna, in the county of Elgin, and accused of arson. The chief witnesses against him were Chisholm and an acquaintance of his named Bloom. He was convicted chiefly on their evidence, and was sentenced to seven years in the Penitentiary. I heard about it and made inquiries, and satisfied myself that Spellman was innocent. I interested County Judge Hughes, and finally had the tailor pardoned, after he served a considerable length of time. Meanwhile Chisholm had landed back in the clutches of the law himself. The same old charge was against him—horse-stealing. He was convicted and sentenced under another name.

"About this time the Government began to receive letters regularly from an inmate of the Penitentiary regarding crimes that had been committed. A day or two after any big burglary or murder or other crime occurred, a letter would come from Kingston Penitentiary offering to reveal the names of the perpetrators. In 1876 an obstruction was placed on the tracks of the Canada Southern Railroad, and in the wreck that followed Engineer Billy Hunt was killed. Three days later came a letter to the Government, and a letter also to the solicitor of the Canada Southern, signed James Clark, from the correspondent in Kingston Penitentiary. Both letters were turned over to me. Clark offered to reveal the names and get the evidence to convict those who did the job. I told the Government officials that I did not believe the letter, but I went to Kingston and the Warden sent for James Clark. Who walked in but old Chisholm! I looked at him as he hopped blithesomely along, and I could hardly keep from laughing.

"'What is your name?' I asked.

"'James Clark,' said he.

"'This is your correspondence?' I asked, producing various letters to the Government on numerous cases.

"'Yes, I wrote them,' said he.

"'Chisholm,' said I, 'you are as big a fraud as you ever were.'

"Old Chisholm stared with open mouth. Then he slapped me on the shoulder.

41

"'Murray, be a man! Be a man!' he said. 'Liberty is sweet. Don't betray me.'

"'Chisholm,' said I, 'I could forgive you everything if you had not sent Spellman, the tailor, to the Penitentiary for burning that barn, when you know he didn't do it.'

"'Oh no, oh no. He did do it,' insisted the lying old rascal.

"'Well, Chisholm, I intend to put a stop to your writing all over the country with these bunko letters,' said I. 'I'll tell the Warden not to send out any more of them. Try to get pardoned some other way, but stop trying to put up jobs to land innocent men in prison simply in hope of getting yourself out.'

"Old Chisholm looked at me sadly.

"'And to think, I thought you were a man, Murray,' he said. 'I honestly thought you were a man. Here am I, in prison, giving you a chance to be a man and get me out, and you won't take it. Well, well, Murray. I'm disappointed in you.'

"I left him wagging his head in seeming sorrow. But he did not stop writing letters. He wrote as before, immediately after hearing of a crime. Nothing was done anywhere in the criminal line, but old Chisholm, upon hearing of it, wrote a letter stating he knew the very man or men who did it. He always added a postscript after my visit. It read : 'Don't tell Murray about this.'

"He got out when his term expired. He stole some more horses and promptly went back again. When arraigned and asked to state his residence, Chisholm answered : 'The Penitentiary.' In truth he spent two-thirds of his sixty years there. Even then, he was away from home about ten years too much. A man like Hunker Chisholm should stay at home indoors about fifty out of sixty years.

"I met later an old, old man who had been Chisholm's teacher in his boyhood. He told me that at school Chisholm stole slate pencils from every one. He stole nothing but slate pencils. When kept in after school or about to be punished he invariably informed the schoolmaster that there was a plot on foot among some of the other pupils to do mischief, and if he was not punished he would tell who the plotters were. This worked at first, and several times innocent boys were punished, just as the innocent tailor, Spellman, was sent to prison. But eventually the schoolmaster got on to Chisholm, although Chisholm kept it up to his last day of school life. The slate pencils of his boyhood symbolised the horses of his manhood."

8

THE MONAGHAN MURDER

FENCE-RAIL robberies were quite a fad in part of Canada early in 1876. The robbers selected isolated houses, in the farming districts, where occupants were prosperous and apt to have money on the premises. In the night the robbers would drive up near the house, take a stout fence-rail, batter in the door, with loud shouts, terrify the family into submission and ransack the rooms, after threatening the family with death, if they did not tell where the money and valuables were concealed. The robbers then would drive away with their plunder, notifying the family they would return and shoot them like dogs if they dared to give an alarm. Old folk usually were the victims.

"In March 1876," says Murray, "there were living in the township of Harwick, county of Lambton, two brothers, Patrick Monaghan and Michael Monaghan, sturdy old Irishmen, both over fifty, and within a few years of the same age. They were bachelors, prosperous and industrious. Their widowed sister, Mrs. McGuire, kept house for them. About March 10th a big snowfall came, and the Monaghan brothers went early to bed and soon were asleep. They occupied the one bed. An old rifle hung above the bed on the wall. It had not been fired for over five years.

"A crash at the front door awakened them in the dead of night. It was followed by shouts and curses, then another crash, and the front door banged open and in rushed three strange men.

"'Get down on your knees!' they shouted with oaths.

"Michael Monaghan leaped out of bed, grabbed the old rifle and rushed to meet them. They met face to face in the big room, in the darkness save for the flash of their lantern.

44

They saw a figure in white, with a long rifle pointed at them.

"'Stand back and get out!' commanded the figure.

"A second white figure with an axe loomed up as Patrick joined Michael.

"'Out, or I'll shoot!' said Michael.

"A revolver spat a flash of flame in the darkness. Michael fell, shot through the leg. The robbers fled. Patrick bent over Michael.

"'Good-bye, Pat, I'm done for,' said Michael.

"The bullet had cut an artery in Michael's leg and he bled to death. I was detailed by the Government at once. I drove to the Monaghans, and there I tramped all around the house and the road in the heavy snow of the day of the murder. I came upon the track of a cutter that had been hitched not far from the house. No neighbours had hitched a cutter there. Tracks led from it to the fence, where a rail had been taken, and thence the tracks led to the Monaghan house and then back to the cutter.

"I took the trail of the cutter. A piece evidently had been broken out of the shoe of the cutter for it left a mark on the snow as if it had been split. I observed also a pecular mark in the print of a foot of one of the horses. Evidently it interfered for it had been shod so that a crossbar showed singularly on the shoe. With these two marks to identify the trail, I started at once. I went to Brantford and followed the tracks to London, to the house of a woman known as Mary Ann Taylor. I followed also the tracks of the cutter as it drove to the Monaghan farm over twenty-five miles from London. In Brantford I immediately set out to find the cutter. In the stable of Liveryman Hewart I found a Portland cutter that had a split about six inches long in the hind part of the shoe. In searching the cutter we found the shell of a cartridge that fitted the bullet found in Monaghan's leg. I learned that three men hired a team in the evening. They wanted two good travellers. A cross-matched pair, one white and one black, were offered. They objected to taking the white horse, and a dark bay horse was substituted.

45

They drove that night to London, over forty miles away and the horses were put up at Lewis's Hotel in London.

"Mary Ann Taylor had no information to give me. Among the girls who lived in her house was a very pretty German girl named Polly Ripple. She came from Brooklyn in the State of New York. I learned that three men had stopped at Mary Ann Taylor's and had some beer and then drove on along the road that led to Monaghan's. I found a witness who saw three men in a cutter at Hickory Corners, a few miles out on the way. On the night of the murder, Polly Ripple was late for the midnight meal at Mary Ann Taylor's, and she said Mary Ann was serving three men. Polly swore she saw them and heard them mimic the Irishmen, Monaghan.

" ' Arrah, Mike, are you shot ? ' the one was saying.

" ' Shure, I am, Pat,' said another.

" The upshot of all my work was the arrest in London of Daniel MacPhee and Robert Murray, and the arrest in Brantford on May 15th, 1876, of Robert Greeny. On May 18th they were committed to Sarnia gaol to stand trial. Before the trial, Polly Ripple disappeared. I went to her old home in Brooklyn and through her friends there I located her in Rochester, where she was living with a Mrs. Jennings. I went to Rochester to see her, but pretty Polly said she would not go back to Canada for all the diamonds in the world. I could not take her back. So I set out to get her back by strategy. I learned the name of a young fellow in Rochester on whom pretty Polly was sweet. I quickly got in with him and arranged for him to take pretty Polly to Niagara Falls on an excursion. When they arrived at the Falls they crossed to the Canada side to get a better view of the cataract, and pretty Polly was taken in charge by a respectable woman who made sure she would be present at the trial.

" Bob Murray, who was a big fine-looking fellow, of respectable family, got out on bail and did not appear for trial. In those days I could not get them back from the States, as I could later. At the trial Arthur Sturgis Hardy, the late Premier of the Province, then a Queen's Counsel and a Member of Parliament, defended the prisoners, and the present Judge MacMahon was prosecutor. Mr. Hardy and I had quite a tiff at this trial and it was some months before we made peace. But we became good friends and later he became Attorney-General and head of the Department of Justice.

"When pretty Polly Ripple came to tell her story on the stand I cautioned her to tell the truth, the naked truth. She did not vary from her story of the men in Mary Ann Taylor's and she saw them plainly and heard them mimic the Monaghans. Mr. Hardy's cross examination of her dealt with details of her life in Mary Ann Taylor's, and she answered truthfully about the life of shame, and some of its particular degradations, and the judge became disgusted. I pitied poor, pretty Polly, who told the naked truth. Greeny and McPhee were acquitted. Bob Murray was not tried, as he was shot and killed in Port Huron by a fellow named Tom Britton, a brother of Royal Britton. Tom Britton was not convicted for the shooting, and he, too, is dead. Dan McPhee went to Australia ; he was a horseman. Greeny is a hotel-keeper in the United States. He is one of the men in this world who do not feel kindly towards me.

"After the Monaghan affair it was a long time before I heard of another fence-rail robbery, and it was not in this part of the world at all. So far as Greeny and McPhee were concerned their acquittal of course established, in the eyes of the law, their innocence. Pretty Polly Ripple went back to the United States, and Mary Ann Taylor was as uncommunicative in after years as she was in 1876, and compared with Mary Ann at that time an oyster was loquacious and a clam was a garrulous, talkative thing."

9

THE FATAL ROBBERY OF THE DAINS

WHILE crimes were occurring in the counties round about Toronto, the capital city was not immune. On a bitter cold night, in March 1875, two men slipped noiselessly along in the darker shadow of the house walls in Yonge Street. One was on one side of the street, the other was on the other side of the street. They made their way swiftly and silently out to the corner of Bloor Street, where the city limits ended in those days, and the district beyond was called York. On a corner of Yonge and Bloor streets lived the Dains. They were rich drovers and butchers. Three brothers— Joseph Dain, James Dain, and Major Dain—lived there with their mother. They were good business men, and carried large sums of money on their person for cattle buying.

Their house loomed silent and sombre in the night. The two men in the street met in its shadow, and slipped around to the rear. One of the two took his stand by the rear corner of the house, where he could see any one approaching. The other took off his overcoat, handed it to him, and approached the door. He fumbled in his pocket a moment and produced something that resembled a double-sized cigar. He pressed it close against the door. There was a moment's silence, then a rending sound, and the door swung open. He had jemmied it. Both men waited, but no noise from within followed the forcing of the door. The one man noiselessly entered the house, and the other moved in and stood by the doorway, concealed from any passer-by. Upstairs Joseph Dain was asleep in his room, his trousers on the chair beside his bed. He stirred, opened his eyes, and saw a tall figure standing by his bed, rifling the pockets of his trousers, in which he had considerable money. Joseph Dain was a

48

powerful, fearless man, and he leaped out of bed and grabbed the burglar. The man broke away and fled downstairs, where his pal was waiting. As he bounded down the stairs his pal swung the door wide open, and as he sprang past, his pal slammed the door in the face of Joseph Dain, and the two burglars fled, separating as they ran.

Dain jerked open the door, and although there was snow on the ground, and it was almost zero weather, and he was naked, save for a night-shirt, he gave chase to the man who was running down Bloor Street West. It was the one who had rifled his trousers. Block after block they ran, and Dain, his feet bare and bleeding, was gaining on his man when the burglar shouted over his shoulder:

" Turn back or I'll shoot!"

Dean leaped forward, and was closing on him when a shot rang out, and Dain fell with a bullet in the abdomen. The burglar pocketed a smoking revolver, ran on, and escaped.

His pal meanwhile, as he ran across Yonge Street, tripped on the extra overcoat he was carrying, and fell. A baker going to work in the early morning hours, grabbed the fallen man, and held him until a policeman came and locked him up. Dain was carried indoors, surgeons were summoned, and he rallied after the operation for the bullet.

" I did not take up the case until later, when I looked the captured burglar over, and recognised him at once as Charles Leavitt, a desperate American burglar and thief," says Murray. " His home was Buffalo, although the police there knew him so well that it was the last place he could hope to stay. I took the overcoat, and looked it over carefully, and found in it the mark of a Cleveland tailor. I started for Cleveland, and, in looking up Leavitt's record in the States, I found that one of his friends was Frank Meagher, of Cleveland, a dangerous man, a skilled burglar, a clever crook, and one of the ablest and worst rough-ones at large at that time. I knew his description well. It tallied in general outline with Dain's description of the burglar at his bedside. It tallied exactly with the tailor's description of the man for whom he made the coat. The escaped burglar, I was satisfied, was Frank Meagher. He and Leavitt, a bold and reckless pair, had crossed to Canada on a burglary tour, and had spotted the Dain house for their first job.

"Meagher seemed to have vanished completely. I set out to trace him in Toronto after the shooting. I made the rounds of all the resorts, and finally found a young man named John Jake Ackermann. Jake was known in Toronto as Keno Billy, and was a bar-tender and faro dealer. He was at a place on King Street, known as the Senate saloon, kept by Mike Ganley, a United States refugee from justice in Indiana, when Meagher arrived on the day of the burglary. Jake had taken Meagher's valise and put it behind the bar. About an hour after Dain was shot, Meagher appeared at the back door of the Senate, and was admitted by Bill Frazer, one of Ganley's friends, and then the trail disappeared. Ganley's place was a great hang-out in those days for men of Meagher's stripe.

"Leavitt was convicted, and was sentenced to Kingston Penitentiary for life. He took his medicine without a word, refused to betray his pal, and went, with sealed lips, to serve until death inside the prison walls. No trace could be found of Meagher.

"Dain did not die immediately. He lived over one year and one day. Under the law in England and Canada, a man cannot be convicted of murder and hanged, if his victim lives for one year and one day after the crime is committed. Dain lived for a couple of months over the year and died. The wound inflicted by Meagher caused hernia of the bowels, and killed him. But he died too late to hang the murderer even if he could be found. I determined to find Meagher if it took twenty years.

"Two years passed. I searched on. Whenever I made a trip to any big police centre I made special enquiries. I examined every description I could obtain of every prisoner sentenced to any prison in Canada or the States. In 1877 I came across a description that fitted Meagher in almost every respect. It was of a man sentenced to seven years' imprisonment in the Northern Indiana Penitentiary for a burglary at Big Bend under the name of Louis Armstrong. I read it over and over, and the oftener I read it the surer I became that Louis Armstrong was none other than Frank Meagher. I prepared extradition papers, and on June 1st, 1877, I started for Indianapolis. Detective Lou Muncie, of Cleveland, who knew Meagher well by sight, went out to the prison and identified him, and thus I made doubly sure that Armstrong was Meagher, for the moment I saw him I was satisfied of it.

"When I arrived in Indianapolis I called on my old friend, General McAuley, formerly of Buffalo, and then Mayor of Indianapolis. General McAuley had a twin brother, by the way, and they looked as much like one another as did the Needhams. The General said to me that the man for me to see was 'Dan Voorhees, of Terre Haute, one of the best criminal lawyers in this state.' I also called on my friend, Senator Joseph E. MacDonald, who corroborated General McAuley. I went to Terre Haute, and stated my case to Voorhees. I told him that the State of Indiana had a criminal serving a sentence for a crime committed subsequent to the commission of a far graver crime in Canada, and that I wanted to take him back at once to pay the penalty of his prior crime. Voorhees took the case, and accompanied me to Indianapolis, and there the fine point of law was raised.

"Meagher was a man serving a term in a penitentiary in the State of Indiana, paying a penalty he owed the State for burglary. Could he be taken out of the State before he paid that penalty? Blue Jean Williams, the farmer who wore Kentucky blue jean, was Governor. Voorhees had stumped the State for him. We called on him, and also on former Governor Tom Hendricks, later nominated for Vice-President, and on former Governor Baker, who agreed with Voorhees that they would sanction Meagher's return to stand trial in the country where he committed the greatest offence. We called also on Judge Gresham, later Postmaster General, who suggested to Voorhees that he should see Chief Justice· Perkins of the Indiana Courts. We called on Chief Justice Perkins, who heard the statement of the case from Voorhees. and said that if it was laid before him in due form he would call in his associate judges and consult them on the matter, He did so, and they suggested that the Governor should serve a writ of habeas corpus on the Warden of the Northern Indiana Penitentiary to produce Meagher before the Supreme Court of the State. This was done.

"The Warden produced Meagher in Indianapolis. The prisoner was taken before the full bench of state judges. I went on the stand, and was sworn as the representative of the Canadian Government, and stated and proved the case of the Crown against Meagher. A Cleveland detective identified Armstrong as Meagher. Meagher had counsel, and a long argument followed. Voorhees made the claim that the country where the first and greatest crime was committed should have preference in the custody of the prisoner. Chief Justice Perkins suggested that the Governor might issue a conditional pardon. The court sent a transcript of the proceedings to the State Department in Washington, and on June 19th, 1877, a warrant of surrender was sent to me in Indianapolis. The Governor had granted a conditional pardon on June 8th, and Meagher was ordered into my custody.

"Meagher was in gaol in Indianapolis, where he was kept pending the outcome of the case. He got wind of the conditional pardon and of the case going against him. He was a bad man, a clever and daring crook. Two or three times in his career he had escaped, and had shot and killed a deputy on one occasion. He had a brother, Charlie Meagher, of Cleveland, also a thief and burglar—a desperate, resourceful crook. He had friends ; and Frank Meagher, then a fine-looking, well-educated fellow of twenty-eight, was highly respected and much liked among the abler crooks for his daring and cleverness. I knew that the chances were all in favour of complete plans having been made to rescue Frank. I had all my papers ready on the evening of June 19th. It was long after midnight when I had the last of them signed. I went direct to the gaol with Detective Lou Muncie. A train left at 4.35 o'clock in the morning, and I decided to get away on it with Meagher, and had notified the sheriff several hours before. We arrived at the gaol about three o'clock in the morning.

"'Mr. Sheriff,' said I, 'I am here after Meagher. Here are my papers.'

"'I'm afraid we're going to have trouble with Meagher,' said the sheriff, who was greatly perturbed.

"'What's the trouble with Meagher?' said I.

"'He's armed, and he's got up to the fourth floor, the top tier of cells, and threatens to kill any one who goes near him,' said the sheriff with the perspiration streaming down his face. 'He's a desperate man, Mr. Murray; a desperate man.'

"'Sheriff,' said I, 'I want the prisoner. My papers call on you to produce the prisoner.'

"'But how am I to produce him?' exclaimed the worried sheriff.

"'That is for you to determine,' said I. 'Please produce the prisoner.'

"'Well, then, come this way, please,' said the sheriff; and we went into the main part of the gaol, where the cells rose in four tiers, with iron stairways leading up from tier to tier.

"The sheriff looked up to the top tier, and there, at the head of the stairway, sat Meagher. He had a baseball bat in one hand and a revolver in the other.

"'Meagher, come down!' called the sheriff in nervous voice.

"Meagher's answer was a volley of oaths.

"'Come up and get me!' he yelled. 'I'll kill the first —— that sets foot on these stairs!'

"'There, you see!' said the sheriff to me.

"'Sheriff, I want him,' said I. 'Here are the documents. It's your duty to produce him.'

"The sheriff was in a sad state of mind.

"'I know! I know!' he exclaimed. 'But I don't want to be killed or to see anybody else get killed.'

"I saw that the sheriff would not get Meagher. I saw also that Meagher was playing for time, and the purpose of it probably was an attempt to rescue him. From the fact that he had the revolver and club, I knew that some of his pals were at work. I decided that I must take him on the 4.35 train at all hazards.

"'Open that gate,' I said to the sheriff. 'I want to speak to him.'

"'Don't do it,' said the sheriff. 'He'll kill you!'

"'John, I wouldn't do it,' said Muncie.

"'I warn you not to go,' said the sheriff.

"I had him open the gate. I stepped in and walked upstairs. When I reached the landing of the stairs, where Meagher was at the top, he said:

"'Stop, Murray! Don't you come near me!'

"I stopped. I saw the club and the revolver, and he had the gun pointed straight at me. I could see the gloom in the muzzle.

"'I am not coming up, Frank,' I said, as I stood on the stairs. 'I want to talk to you so everybody won't hear.'

"He had risen, and we stood, he at the top of the stairs, I just below him. All was quiet.

"'Come down, or I'll shoot!' shrilly cried the sheriff below.

"I heard Muncie sternly tell the sheriff to shut up.

"'Shoot and be —— !' yelled Meagher to the sheriff. 'I'd rather be shot here than hung in Canada.'

"'Shut up, sheriff,' I said, with my eyes still on Meagher, who, while he yelled defiance to the sheriff, had not swerved his glance for an instant from me. 'Frank,' I continued, 'you won't be hung. You know that. The man lived over a year. You know you've got to come. You could try to kill me, but you would go just the same.'

"While I was speaking I mounted the stairs step by step until I stood within ten feet of him. He stood above me, with the revolver pointed full at me.

"'Stop!' he said. 'Stand where you are! Not a step nearer!'

"I stopped and looked him full in the eye, face to face; and I have a feeling to this day that I never was nearer death in my entire life. He looked me over slowly from head to foot and back again. His eye was cold and hard, yet, as he glared at me, I saw that something of curiosity mingled with its murderous, merciless, fine-pointed blaze. He eyed me thus for several minutes. Neither of us spoke. My hands were empty, my revolver was in my pocket.

54

"'Murray,' he said suddenly, but without shifting his eyes, 'I have no fit clothes. I am not going like a pauper to Canada. I am a gentleman.'

"'The sheriff has a suit of clothes for you, Frank,' I said. 'It's a pretty good suit; but if it is not good enough, I will wait until you can get one.'

"His eye lighted with satisfaction; and I was sure then that he was playing for delay, and I was doubly determined to take him on the 4.35 train. He began to curse Muncie, possibly hoping a row would break out then and there.

"'I don't blame you, Murray,' he said. 'But don't you come near me.'

"I thought it all over. He could kill me as easy one way as another, so I turned my back half to him and sat down on the stair. If he had glanced away I could have slipped out my gun. He watched me like a hawk. I yawned and turned my back full to him.

"'I do not want to get hurt any more than you do, Frank; but I'm not afraid of anything any more than you are,' I remarked.

"There was a long silence. I wondered once if he would reach down and smash me with the club, and I thought I heard a cat-like tread on the step. I kept my eyes front, however, although I have done easier things in my life. Finally he spoke—softly, and in almost a whisper.

"'Murray,' he said, 'you're a game man. Get me a suit of clothes and I'll go with you, but not with Muncie.'

"He handed me the club.

"'Give me the gun, Frank,' said I.

"He handed me the gun. We walked down the stairs into the office side by side. He spat at the sheriff and swore at Muncie, and his glance flew to the clock as we passed it. It was four o'clock, and a smile flitted over his face. He donned the suit of clothes, and he really looked a prosperous gentleman. I put the irons on him, and, with him swearing all the way at Muncie, we drove at a gallop in a closed carriage to the station. As we alighted the train was making ready to go. A second carriage galloped up, and out jumped Red Jim Carroll, Joe Dubuque, and two others of their crowd. I lifted Meagher aboard the train, Muncie beside me. As the train pulled out a third carriage came up, the horses on a gallop; but the carriage door evidently stuck, for the men inside missed the train. Red Jim and his three, however, caught it.

"'See them?' I said to Muncie, as they entered another car.

"He nodded.

"'We're going to have some trouble,' said I.

"Meagher was very nervous. I had leg-irons as well as hand-cuffs on him. I sent for the train conductor and brakeman, and told them I expected trouble.

"'Well, I and my crew are not on this train to get shot, but I'll do what I can,' said the conductor.

"We put Frank in the middle, Muncie facing one way and I the other, with our revolvers in our hands, well beyond Frank's reach.

"'Frank,' I said, 'if there's any break here, some one will get killed before we do.'

"I think he knew what I meant.

"An hour passed. No one entered the car. We had scanned the faces of every one in it, and most of them had hastened into other cars after our talk with the conductor. Suddenly the front door of the car swung open and in stepped Red Jim Carroll. I had told Muncie if they started in, to jump to his feet and fight them standing, for a man is as good a target sitting as standing. We both jumped up as Red Jim entered, Muncie still facing the other way and I facing Red Jim. The others of his crowd were behind him.

"'Stop there, Jim!' I ordered.

"He stopped in the doorway, and it was a wise act.

"'Good morning, Mr. Murray,' he said. 'Good morning,' Mr. Muncie.'

"'Are you looking for trouble, Jim?' said I.

"'No, Mr. Murray, I am not looking for trouble,' he answered, with a grin. 'Will you allow me to speak to Frank?'

"'Speak to him from right there, Jim,' said I.

"Meagher had been watching the whole affair. I had

reminded him that he must sit absolutely quiet in the seat. When Muncie and I rose up he had half risen, but remembered in time and sat back, watching all that occurred with eager, encouraging face turned toward Red Jim. But when Carroll halted Meagher's face grew sullen.

"'Go to hell!' he shouted at Red Jim.

"Jim was about to put a hand in his pocket when I stopped him, for I did not know what he might draw forth, and Meagher's rage could easily have been feigned.

"'What did you want to get, Jim?' I said.

"'I wanted to give Frank a couple of hundred dollars,' said Red Jim.

"'Go to hell with your money!' roared Meagher, who seemingly was in a terrible rage over the failure, thus far, of the plot for his rescue.

"Still keeping Red Jim covered, I told him to go no lower than his breast pocket with his hands, and to count out the money where he stood, and I would take it and see Frank got it. Meagher shouted that he wanted none of the dirty money of a gang of cowards that would stand by and see a friend dragged away.

"Red Jim answered with a touch of dignity.

"'Sometimes the worst comes to the worst, Frank, and nothing can help it just at the time,' said Red Jim. 'This man, Murray, is a gentleman, Frank, and he will take no advantage of you, and he will give you a fair show.'

"So saying, Red Jim tossed the money toward my feet, remarking I would have to pardon him for not handing it to me.

"'Good-bye, Jim,' I said pointedly.

"He hesitated, glanced at me with a revolver in each hand, then nodded.

"'Good-bye, Mr. Murray,' he said. 'Good-bye, Frank. Good-bye, Mr. Muncie.'

"He backed out of the doorway and closed the door. Meagher was beside himself with wrath. I picked up the money Red Jim had left for him, and later I gave it to Frank, and he found it of real use in his defence by able counsel. The train stopped at a junction. I had the brakeman bring

our breakfast aboard.   As the train pulled out Red Jim stood
on the platform and waved good-bye.

"We went through to Buffalo, and thence to Lewiston on
the Niagara River, and thence by boat to Toronto.   As the
steamer passed Old Fort Niagara at the mouth of the river
and glided out into Lake Ontario, Meagher stood on deck.
The American flag was flying over Fort Niagara.   He raised
his manacled hands and saluted the flag.

"'God bless it!' he said.   'I suppose it's the last time I
ever shall see it.   Good-bye!   I'd rather I was dying for it
than for what I am!'

"He gazed after it until it was a mere speck against the
sky.   He still believed he could be hanged for killing Dain.

"Don't talk like that,' I said to him.   'You won't be hung.
English law will treat you fairly.'

"He answered with a gloomy shake of the head.   We
arrived safely in Toronto, and he was locked up for trial.
Dain was dead.   We had to have the evidence of Leavitt to
convict Meagher.   Leavitt, however, was sentenced for life,
and, being a life prisoner, he was not a competent witness.
He was dead in the eyes of the law, and could not testify.
I went to Kingston and saw Leavitt.   He yearned for liberty,
and I told him we had Meagher beyond doubt.   So I
returned to Toronto, and recommended to the Government
that Leavitt's sentence should be commuted to imprisonment
for ten years, to make him a competent witness.   This was
done.   I took Leavitt from Kingston before the police
magistrate, and also took the notorious Jimmy Pape, pick-
pocket and sneak-thief.   Pape had told a cock-and-bull story
in Kingston about what he knew of the case, but his evidence
simply was that he met Meagher in Chicago, and gave him
some money to go to South America.   I hustled Jimmy
Pape back to Kingston Penitentiary.

"I got a breath of fresh air just the same,' said Jimmy on
the way back.   'I had to get it or die.   I'd lie for it any
time.'

"Leavitt told the story of the crime, and the evidence
corroborated it.   When Meagher heard Leavitt testify he
stood up and swore a savage oath.

"'You traitor!' he said. 'I will kill you in this world or the next.'

"When it came to the trial Keno Billy, otherwise Jake Ackermann, who had taken Meagher's valise for him at the Senate, was missing. He had gone to the States. I went to Buffalo, and there met Bill Carney, who kept the Little Tammany. With Carney I went to New York, and used every effort to get track of Keno Billy, dead or alive. If he was alive, I wanted him to testify. If they had killed him I wanted to know it. I turned out the Police Department in New York, and I got the gamblers and sports, Billy Tracy, Arthur Stanley, and others, and hunted all over, but could find no trace of Keno Billy. Some of Leavitt's friends joined in the hunt, for they felt that, if Meagher was convicted Leavitt would get out. They all failed to find him. Keno Billy was dead to the world in which he had lived.

"I finally set out alone, and came across a man named Ackermann, caretaker and warden for a nice little church on 34th Street, not far from Broadway, in New York. The name was not in the City Directory, but it was on a name plate, and I read it as I passed. A drowning man will clutch at straws, and I walked into the basement of the church to look for Keno Billy, the faro dealer. I found a nice old lady, and I asked for the Ackermann family, and whether they had a son John Jake Ackermann. The old lady burst into tears.

"'Dear me! dear me!' she sobbed. 'You are looking for my dear boy Billy!'

"Even she called him Billy, thought I.

"'Yes,' I answered her. 'But I mean him no harm. Is he here?'

"'No,' said she, sobbing afresh.

"'Where is he?' I asked.

"'Dead and buried four weeks ago yesterday,' said she.

"'Did he die a natural death?' I asked.

"'He did,' said she. 'He just naturally died.'

"I sat down and sympathised with her until she showed me the record of his death, and I then went to verify it. Keno Billy indeed was dead. I returned to Toronto without him.

"Chief Justice Hagerty presided at Meagher's trial. Matthew Cruiks Cameron, an able lawyer, afterwards judge, defended him. The defence was an alibi. They swore Jimmy O'Neill from Detroit, Tom Daly, and some women, but it did not work. Meagher was convicted of robbery, and on January 9th, 1878, he was sentenced to eighteen years in Kingston Penitentiary. He served his time, and the last I heard of him he was near Cleveland. Leavitt was pardoned, after Meagher's conviction, on my suggestion that it would not be safe for him to stay in Kingston, as other convicts probably would kill him. Leavitt behaved for a time, and then showed up in Buffalo, and Chief of Detectives Cusack promptly drove him out. His father was respectable, but Charlie always was a bad one. Of course he worshipped me after regaining his liberty. But some time in this world, or the next, he and Meagher will meet. What a meeting it will be!"

10

"AMER! AMER! AMER!"

FAR to the north, over three hundred miles from Toronto as the crow flies, in the waters of Georgian Bay is Manitoulin Island. Through the township of Tekemah, on this island, winds a road that was famous in years past for the beauty of its scenery. Twenty-five years ago the houses along this road were few and far between. Neighbours usually were from seven to ten miles apart. Here and there two families lived within a mile of one another, but in the outlying sections of the township this was the exception and not the rule. The settlers cleared the land and wrestled with the earth, carving farms out of the wilds. They were a rugged folk, courageous and patient in their struggle with untamed nature.

One Sunday morning in 1877 a young girl of the family of Porters set out to attend church twelve miles away. It was a bright sunshiny June morning and the Tekemah road stretched away like a broad band of ribbon upon which the sunlight and shadows beneath the trees flung a web of finespun lace. The girl was singing as she crossed the crest of the hill and moved down the road where it swept in graceful curve past the home of William Bryan, nearest neighbour to the Porters. Bryan was a good neighbour, a steadfast friend and ready helper. He was a little, old fellow with a squeaky voice and hair the colour of a roan horse. He weighed less than one hundred and thirty-five pounds, but was wiry and active, and there were tales of grand battles he had fought in the days of his youth. He lived with his wife and son Charlie, a young fellow of steady habits and about thirty years old. Mrs. Bryan was a tot of a woman, a mere mite, who seemed to grow smaller year after year, until old age threatened to shrivel her into nothingness, and when she died she would vanish, leaving no body for burial. She was weak in her mind, and was given to spells of blackness, like the long, long nights a little farther north. Their home stood near the road, so situated that a passer-by could hail in easy voice those in the doorway or the yard.

The Porter girl came swinging down the hill. Mrs. Bryan had a habit of joining in any noise she heard, and once or twice the girl in the road paused to hear if the wee woman with the troubled mind had heard her singing and joined in. No answering voice greeted her, so she moved on until, in a rise in the road, she came full upon the Bryan home.

In the doorway sat the faded, shrunken little woman of the troubled mind. Her hair was loose and dangled about her face and down upon her shoulders. She was crooning and swaying to and fro. At times she paused, threw back her head, shook the long hair from her face and laughed a cackling, merry chortle. Again, she bowed her head and wrung her hands and tore her hair and wept and moaned. Then she grew quiet again and mechanically swayed and crooned, and gazed vacantly out upon her little world. The Porter girl, still singing, waved to her and drew near. The little woman of the troubled mind began to mutter and to grin. She waved the singer back with frantic gesture. The girl glanced about the yard and beheld two figures prone and still. One was old man Bryan, the other was his son. The old man's face was upturned, and his eyes gazed dully toward the sky. The son lay face downward, arms extended.

The girl rushed into the yard and gazed first at the father, then at the son. They were dead, with blood dyeing the earth beneath them. The girl turned to the little old woman, who sat in the doorway, tangling her hair.

" How did it happen ? " asked the girl.

The little old woman gazed at her and burst into rippling laughter.

" Amer ! Amer ! Amer ! " she laughed.

" When did it happen ? " asked the girl.

The little old woman laughed on.

" Amer ! Amer ! Amer ! " she said.

It was all that she would say. The girl questioned her closely but no other word passed her lips.

"Amer! Amer! Amer!"

Sometimes she sobbed it, sometimes she laughed it, sometimes she muttered it solemnly.

Back to her own home sped the Porter girl and told her family of the tragedy, and back to the Bryan farm went the Porters; and while some cared for the bodies, others hastened for the coroner and other neighbours. Suspicion inevitably fell upon the little old woman of the troubled mind. Yet her whole life was one of gentleness. She had been known to sob when a chicken was killed, to weep when a cat caught a mouse, or to cry out if her son struck one of the horses with a whip. In the perplexity of the affair, the Department of Justice was notified, and Murray, who had just returned from a trip on the Meagher case, was directed to take it up. He went to Manitoulin Island at once.

"I drove out to the Bryan homestead," says Murray. "There sat the old woman in the doorway, her chickens feeding around her, a cat beside her, a dog at her feet. Some wild birds were fluttering about as if she had been feeding them, or as if they knew her and had no fear. I went to her gently and sat down on the step.

" 'Amer! Amer! Amer!' she murmured softly.

" 'And where is Amer?' I asked very gently.

"She looked cautiously round about, then moved the cat back lest it should hear, and leaned over and whispered in my ear:

" 'Amer! Amer! Amer!'

"I spent an hour or more with the poor little lady and all that she could say was this one word. The dog kept nosing my hand and I shoved him away and bade him sternly to sit down. She wept when I spoke gruffly to the hound.

" The bodies had been buried. The coroner who had made the post-mortem was at Manitowanning. In making the post-mortem he had cut his hand and blood poisoning set in and the results of the post-mortem were not satisfactory, so when the bodies were exhumed I had a second post-mortem made. The bodies bore the marks of heavy blows and both father and son had been killed by bullets. Clearly there had been a fight with strong men and it had culminated in revolver shots. It eliminated the little old woman from any part in the affair. Moreover, I took her muttered word as the clue to solve the case.

"'Amer!' she had muttered.

"On a farm adjoining that of the Bryans lived George Amer and his son Reuben. Their house was less than a mile from the Bryan farm. I began a systematic visiting of all the families thereabouts. I learned that Amer and Bryan had trouble over their boundary line and the line fences, and about the Amer cattle getting in and injuring the Bryan crops. Amer was a big fellow, massive and strong. He formerly was chief constable of Owen Sound. His son Reub was about twenty-four years old and of medium build. I learned from a passing neighbour that, on the day before the Porter girl had found the Bryans dead in their yard, the Amer horses had broken into Bryan's wheatfield, and Bryan and his son impounded them, and were seen tying them up in their yard on that Saturday afternoon of June 8th, 1877. When young Amer went to look for the horses on Saturday night they were gone and he followed their trail from the Bryan wheatfield to the Bryan yard. He went home and reported to his father, who armed himself with a policeman's club that he kept in the house, while the son took a revolver. I found a neighbour who saw them skulking along near the Bryan yard on this Saturday night.

"What happened then only the poor little old woman saw, and she could not testify. But afterwards I learned that the Amers demanded their horses. The Bryans refused to give them up, saying they were impounded. A fight ensued. Big Amer grappled with little Bryan and the wiry old fellow was getting the best of Amer, who called to his son Reub. Young Bryan was struggling with Reub, who, when he heard his father's cry, pulled his revolver and shot and killed both Bryans, and as they lay dead he emptied the revolver into them. Then the Amers took their horses and went home.

"I had the Amers arrested and committed to Sault

Ste. Marie gaol for trial. The regular Assizes were held only once a year there, so the Government commissioned Judge McCrea to try the case. Amer was a man who was rich for that section of the country. He sent to Toronto and employed the Hon. Matthew Cruiks Cameron, paying him a big fee and all expenses. John Hamilton, later a judge and now dead, prosecuted as the Crown Attorney for that district. After reading the depositions, Mr. Cameron told his clients the case would be thrown out by the grand jury. I differed from him. The case was wholly and purely a case of circumstantial evidence, but the chain of circumstances was so complete as to be absolutely convincing. The grand jury took this view and found a true bill. The motive of ill-feeling and the fight over the horses was shown. The evidence showing the Amers approaching the scene of the crime shortly before the murder was presented. The Amers were tried and convicted entirely upon circumstantial evidence. In September 1877 they were sentenced to be hanged.

"Mr. Cameron, for the Amers, filed an objection to the legality of the Court that tried them. He claimed the Government had no authority to commission a judge to try a case of murder. The question was carried to the Divisional Court and to the Court of Appeal, and it was held that the commission was legal and right. The sentence of the Amers was commuted to life imprisonment. Some years afterward, on a strong petition, and aided by political friends, father and son were released, and the last I heard of them they were back on the island where the crime occurred.

"The little old woman, of course, was not called as a witness, as she was not competent. I tried to glean some of the details from her after the arrest of the Amers. I even rehearsed part of the struggle in the yard. She sat in the doorway and screamed with childish delight. Then her mood changed. She dropped her face in her hands.

"'Amer! Amer! Amer!' she sobbed, her hair hanging over her like a veil as she crouched and writhed.

"And 'tis so I see her still, doddering in the doorway."

11

McPHERSON'S TELLTALE TROUSERS

MURRAY was at Manitoulin Island, clearing up details of the Amer case, when a telegram notified him of another murder in the township of Pickering, county of Ontario. It was four hundred miles or more from Tekemah, but the next day Murray drove up the Pickering Road, thirty miles from the railroad, to the house where the murder occurred.

"It was a little house in a lonely part of the township," says Murray. "A labouring farmer, named Bennett, lived there with his wife and two small children. Mrs. Bennett was a pretty woman about thirty years old. Her husband was away working in June, 1877, and she was alone in the house with her two little ones. About midnight two men broke into the house and treated her so horribly, in the presence of the little children, that she died three days later. Her children were too small to be able to tell about the crime. Mrs. Bennett, however, rallied, and described the two men minutely, and finally, in her ante-mortem statement, she said they were two young men named Burk and McPherson, sons of well-known farmers in that vicinity.

"I saw at once that, with the woman dead and her children too young to testify, we would have nothing but her ante-mortem statement ; and while it was strong and convincing the accused had friends, and they were rallying to make a desperate fight, with scores of living against a dead woman's word. I laid my plans.

"Burk and McPherson were arrested. I had them separated at once, and then had each state in detail his movements on the day and night of the murder of Mrs. Bennett. I accepted all they said in apparent credulity. Their confidence grew as they saw me seem to weaken in any belief that they were guilty of the crime. They lied beautifully, lied valiantly, lied so completely that I knew I had them where their word on the witness stand would be blasted and worthless. However, I noted carefully the movements of each as he dictated them. Then I compared them. They vowed they were not together at certain hours, and were in certain places at certain times. I set out and spent days in following these fictitious movements of these two men. I disproved them, step by step. I found people who saw them together when they averred they were apart. I found people who saw them in places where they stoutly maintained they had not been. In short, I incapacitated the pair as worthy witnesses. I had them ; so the word of one dead woman was better than the word of the two live men.

" I searched their houses and the premises round about for evidence that would corroborate the dead woman's word. Hid away in McPherson's mother's house, John Hodgins, one of our Toronto officers, found a pair of his trousers. They were of a kind very fashionable then, but would appear rather ridiculous now. They were light woollen, washable and very baggy, in fact, balloon-like in their leg effects. They had been washed. I took them out in the sunlight, and despite the washing I detected what I believed were stains. McPherson's trousers were taken to Professor Ellis, then assistant to Professor Crofts, at the School of Practical Science in Toronto. He analysed the stain and discovered it was blood, and further that it was the blood of a woman.

" The trial was postponed, but finally held in May 1878, at Whitby. Chief Justice Harrison presided. B. B. Britton, now a judge, prosecuted for the Crown. The Hon. Matthew Cruiks Cameron defended. Mr. Cameron, as in the Amer case, told his clients the grand jury would not find a true bill, Again he was mistaken. It was a tedious trial. We swore many witnesses to trace their movements and contradict them flatly in their story of where they had been on the day of the tragedy. When McPherson's stained trousers were produced they swore in rebuttal that McPherson had killed a rat, and that the bloodstains were the stains of rat's blood, and not of woman's blood. Dr. Ellis positively swore the stains were not rat's blood. The jury so believed, and Burk and McPherson were found guilty and sentenced to be hanged on June 14th, 1878. Both sentences, however, were commuted to life imprisonment, and after both had served long terms they got out.

" Interest in this case grew and became widespread in the States and Canada, because of the point of chemical analysis involved. It was one of the most advanced cases known at that time. It was expert testimony, of course, but it was founded on a precise science, and therefore certain and accurate. Some expert testimony becomes largely a matter of opinion, but that opinion is based on trained judgment, skilled discernment, and scientific methods for ascertaining the truth. Experts may differ honestly, and here and there an expert or two may differ otherwise. But the testimony of competent experts, known to be men of ability and integrity, like Dr. Ellis, is as valuable as the testimony of worthless witnesses is valueless.

" At this time I was opposed in three prominent cases by the Hon. Matthew Cruiks Cameron. They were the Meagher case, the Amer case, and the Burk and McPherson case. In each case he defended. He was the greatest criminal lawyer in those days. Almost invariably he appeared for the accused. Later he became a judge, and died in the fulness of his powers and fame. When a judge he seemed to feel instinctively that he was concerned in the prisoner's defence. Hence he was not always very satisfactory to the prosecution in a criminal case, yet he was an able man. It was force of habit asserting itself unconsciously, and was not intentional partiality, for he was a man of integrity.

" Judges run that way, just as do men in other walks of life. Early training asserts itself in the judge's career on the bench, particularly in regard to his attitude towards persons accused of crime. Perhaps I should say his point of view, rather than his attitude. The point of view of each of us is our view point, or the position from which we view a matter, and that position is determined by our career up to the time we come to consider the case presented to us. We adjust our views of a criminal case according to our judgment, and my experience is that the judgment of a judge is formed on a foundation in which the corner-stone is the substance of his training prior to going upon the bench.

" The machinery of justice makes few slips, after all. It has a gigantic task, for to it is assigned the perpetual adjustment of human rights and wrongs. If either hand of the blindfolded goddess were to symbolise criminal justice, it is the right hand with the sword. I have seen it strike with the swiftness of a lightning flash. I have seen it hover like the sword of Damocles, suspended by a thread for years before it falls. In these three cases in which the Hon. Matthew Cruiks Cameron was pitted against us, I sometimes think that justice showed its certainty. Years passed in one, a thread of circumstantial evidence held true in another, and truth prevailed in the third ; while in all three justice was done, and the heavens did not fall.

12

THE DISAPPEARING STORES

THE night express from Montreal was puffing into Cornwall, and Murray, who had finished with the case of Louis Kipp, was waiting in the station to return to Toronto, when a telegram was handed to him. It was from George F. Marter, formerly leader of the Conservative or Opposition party in Parliament, and now manager of the Lancashire Insurance Company of Toronto. It simply stated that the general store at Gravenhurst had been cleaned out by unknown thieves.

"A short time before," says Murray, thieves had plundered a harness shop in Gravenhurst. All that remained of the shop was the frame of the building. Every scrap of stock had vanished in a single night ; collars, harness, whips, blankets, everything in the store had been taken. Lettbridge was a little place, six miles from Gravenhurst and about one hundred and thirty miles north of Toronto. Mr. Marter and his partner, Hull, had a timber limit and saw mill there. In connection with the mill in Lettbridge they started a general store in Gravenhurst. The goods were bought at wholesale houses in Montreal and Toronto, and were shipped at Gravenhurst, and delivered into the general store. They were not unpacked, but were still in their boxes when they vanished as the harness shop had vanished. It was in May 1878. I went on through Toronto to Gravenhurst, arriving the next day. Mr. Marter met me and we went to the store. It had been cleared out, big boxes and little boxes ; almost the entire stock had been stolen. My mind went back to the old days in Erie, and I wondered if George Knapp had moved to Canada and settled somewhere in the vicinity of Lettbridge. Knapp was the only man I ever had seen who would feel equal to stealing a harness shop and then a general store.

"I asked Marter to let me talk during the day with all the men in his employ. I went with him to his mill at Lettbridge, and began with the head sawyer and the tail sawyer, and then the teamsters, and then the other men, getting their ideas and opinions, and asking if they knew of any strangers in the vicinity. They all passed muster with me except one fellow, a big teamster named George Rose. His eyes were too small and too quick, and his story was too smooth. He said nothing to cast suspicion on himself. On the contrary his talk was very plausible. But of all the men he was the one whose looks I did not like. I thought him over carefully, and finally I went, alone, to his house. He was married and lived in a house among the rocks, about a mile from the saw mill, in a picturesque, out-of-the-way, inaccessible place. He and his wife and a seven-year-old boy lived there. I hunted around, looking for signs of fresh digging or traces of newly turned earth. I found not a sign, not a clue, not a single thread. Back to Toronto I went, empty handed.

"I turned the case over in my mind night and day. Whenever I thought of it there seemed to rise in my vision the face of Rose, with the sneaky eyes. I kept thinking of him until my suspicion grew to a moral certainty. Back I went to Lettbridge. I went straight to Rose's house and walked in. His wife was there. I spoke of the robbery of Marter's store. She replied it was wonderful to think it could be done. I called the little boy. He was a nice child, with a strong English accent.

"'This is not your boy?' I said to Mrs. Rose, when I heard him speak.

"'Oh no,' said she. 'We adopted him from Miss Rye at Belleville.'

"The lad chatted with me, telling me of the ship on which he came over. I lingered around the house, but neither there nor elsewhere in Lettbridge could I find a trace of the perpetrators of the robbery. It annoyed me. Here was a complete general store, packed in boxes filling many waggons, goods worth thousands of dollars and of great bulk, gone completely, vanished in the night, and not a clue even as to the road they went. They did not fall through the earth. They did not vanish into air. They must have been hauled away, and that meant many waggon loads, and yet there was not a single track nor trail nor trace of their whereabouts or of the road they were taken. The more I hunted for evidence against Rose the less I seemed to find. He and his wife lived happily, and were very fond of their adopted child. I stayed around a day or two and I went away again empty handed.

"At this moment in the case, although I was bare of evidence, I could have sworn almost to a certainty that Rose stole the store. I thought and thought and thought. At last a plan presented itself. I wrote to Miss Rye at Belleville to take the child away. She sent a man at once to Lettbridge to take the boy away from the Roses. I had the man bring the boy to me. I examined him carefully. I found he was wearing new stockings and had two new pocket-handkerchiefs that never had been used.

" 'Where did you get these ? ' I asked him.

" 'My mamma,' said the little fellow, meaning Mrs. Rose. ' She cried when I left.'

"I bought him new stockings and handkerchiefs and some candy and sent him on his way to Miss Rye. I kept the stockings and kerchiefs given to him by Mrs. Rose. Several times I had mentioned Rose to Mr. Marter, who invariably defended and praised the teamster. Time passed. Mr. Marter was worried greatly. No trace of his store had appeared. He came to me the day I saw the boy on his way to Miss Rye.

" 'Any clue, Murray ? ' he asked.

" 'I do not like Rose,' said I.

" 'Nonsense,' said he. ' Rose is all right. He is a good man, a reliable man. He is steady and goes to church.'

" ' That cuts no figure with me,' said I. ' Many a job has been planned by a churchman.'

" 'You should not be swayed in your suspicions by dislike of a man's looks,' said he.

" For answer I showed him the handkerchiefs and stockings.

" ' Did you buy such goods ? ' I asked.

" 'Why, yes, I did ! ' he exclaimed.

72

" I went back to Gravenhurst. I spent a day in the town learning if Rose had any friends there. I found, from residents, that a barber named James Fuller was a great friend of Rose. I waited until next morning, so that my beard would be out, and then went to Fuller's shop to get shaved. Fuller was out. A half-breed woman, his wife, part Indian and part white, was keeping shop. She sat in a back room with the door half open, so she could see who entered the shop. She was sewing lace on some undergarment. A bunch of lace was on the floor beside her. I walked right through the shop into the back room.

" ' Fuller in ? ' I asked.

" ' No, he's gone to Cooksville,' said she.

" ' That's pretty lace ; where did you get it ? ' I asked, picking up a piece of the lace and admiring it.

" ' I bought it at Coburn's store,' said she, with a furtive glance at me.

" ' How much did you pay for it ? ' I asked.

" ' I forget,' said she.

" ' I wonder if they have any more of it,' I said. ' How long ago did you get it ? '

" ' I don't remember,' said she.

" ' May I have this piece as a sample ? ' said I, pocketing the piece I had picked up. ' I want to get some like it.'

" She objected. I walked out of the shop. This was on Saturday, July 13th, 1878. I went to Coburn's store. They said they had sold no lace to Fuller's woman, and when I showed them the piece they said they never had carried such lace.

" I went before a magistrate and laid an information against Rose and Fuller. Fuller had gone to Cooksville. I went out to Lettbridge and met Marter, and told him I was going to arrest Rose. Marter identified the lace, and went with me to Rose's house amid the rocks. Rose sat in the doorway cleaning a breech-loading carbine.

" ' Hello, Rose,' said I. ' What are you doing ? '

" ' Cleaning my gun,' said Rose.

" ' That's a nice-looking gun,' said I. ' Let me see it.'

" He handed me the gun. I laid it aside and arrested him.

He made no resistance and I put the handcuffs on him. He asked what he was arrested for. I told him it was for robbing Marter's stores.

"'We'll see about this,' said Rose, with an air of injured innocence.

"We started for Gravenhurst. We walked part of the way to the station in silence.

"'Rose,' said I, 'the jig is up. See these?' and I drew the lace out of my pocket. 'The squaw is coming out in good style.'

"'What squaw?' asked Rose surlily.

"'Mrs. Fuller?' said I.

"Rose was mum. We walked on in silence for half a mile.

"'Rose,' said I. 'I don't think it is fair for Fuller to throw the responsibility for this job on you. I believe he knows more about it than that you gave him this lace as a present.'

"Rose said nothing until we got out to the railroad track, a mile from his house. Then he broke silence.

"'Fuller has not treated me fairly,' said Rose. 'He lied about the lace. Come on. I'll show you where the stuff is.'

"We went back a mile to his house. A rod or two from the back of his house was a potato patch between two rocks, about twenty feet apart.

"'There it is,' said Rose.

"I stared at the potato patch where the potatoes were growing and the ground was unbroken. I thought he was joking, like old Knapp in Erie about the buried gold. I sternly told him to dig it up if it was there. I loosened the handcuffs. Rose dug down into the potato patch and struck boards. He pulled up one or two of these boards and there, beneath, the potato patch in a big hole or bowl in the earth, was the stolen store. Mr. Marter went for his men and teams while Rose cleared the potato patch away. It was the cleverest hiding-place I had ever seen. He had laid some of Marter's lumber across the opening or mouth of the big hole and had dumped dirt on to the boards and had planted potatoes in this earth, making a garden or potato patch as the covering for the goods. In the two months and more that had passed the potatoes had flourished.

"In addition to finding the stolen general store, we found the stolen harness shop with dozens of sets of harness, collars, saddles, etc. It took Marter's men half the night, to haul the stuff back to the store. Rose threw the blame on Fuller, saying Fuller planned it while Rose simply did the hauling and helped to hide the goods. They had begun on a Saturday night, and spent Saturday and Sunday nights stealing and hauling and hiding the boxes of goods. I locked Rose up.

"Fuller was in Cooksville, eighty miles away. I arranged to block any telegram that might be sent to him and that night I drove over fifty miles to Barrie. There my horse gave out, for it was a choking hot night in July. I hired another team and arrived in Cooksville about eight o'clock in the morning. I tied the team in the hotel shed and turned to walk down the street. I met a fellow on the street by the hotel.

"'Can you direct me to a barber's shop?' I asked.

"'I am going there,' said he. 'I am a barber myself.'

"'Is that so?' said I.

"'Yes,' said he. 'But not here.'

"'Where are you from?' I asked.

"'Gravenhurst,' said he.

"'Oh yes,' said I. 'I think you shaved me there.'

"'Yes, I probably did,' said he. 'My name's Fuller.'

"'Oh yes, Fuller,' said I. 'Well, you'll never shave me again,' and I arrested him.

"He took it very hard. He protested his innocence. I showed him the stockings and the handkerchiefs, but not the lace.

"'Fuller,' said I, 'I don't believe you gave these to George Rose as a present for his adopted boy. I believe Rose knows something about them himself.'

"Thereupon Fuller, wrathful at Rose, told the whole story, cursing Rose while he told it. He said Rose planned the job and got him into it, and that he could not have planned it, for he did not know the country or the store as did Rose.

75

After breakfast I drove with Fuller to Barrie and there took the train to Gravenhurst, arriving at one o'clock on Monday afternoon. Both Rose and Fuller demanded a speedy trial. Both pleaded guilty on Wednesday, July 17th, 1878, and were sentenced to five years each in Kingston Penitentiary. Fuller was the tool. Rose was a bloomer, well named."

13

MARY ANN WEATHERUP, COQUETTE

MARY ANN WEATHERUP was a country coquette. She lived in the township of Hope, in the county of Durham. She was a buxom, blooming girl, with red cheeks and fluffy hair and big eyes. Many a lad in the township of Hope spent long hours in the township of Despair, all on account of Mary Ann Weatherup. She would pick out a young fellow, spoon with him on moonlight nights, drive with him on Sunday afternoon, and when Monday came, he was left to sit on the fence and crack his knuckles, while Mary Ann Weatherup went gaily off with another swain. The youth who basked in Mary Ann's smile for a month plumed himself on his powers of attraction, for seldom did a lover outlast a fortnight in the good graces of Mary Ann Weatherup. Squeaky shoes or pomaded hair or choker collar or city perfume never dazzled Mary Ann Weatherup. She loved variety, and men came and went with unbroken regularity, regardless of the artificial charms with which they were bedecked.

Mary Ann Weatherup's family lived on a little rented farm in a house scarcely large enough for the father and mother and three sisters, of whom Mary Ann was the oldest. They were poor in worldly goods, but Mary Ann was rich in physical beauty. She stayed at home until opportunities came for her to work out, and then she was much away, working at the house of some big farmer. Her admirers ever kept her whereabouts in mind, and it is related that there were evenings on the farm where Mary Ann Weatherup was employed when eleven young men sat moodily on different sections of the same rail fence waiting for Mary Ann to stroll forth in the twilight. It is related also that Mary Ann Weatherup would saunter forth and gracefully trip along the path, glancing at each figure on the fence until she had passed them all. Then, to make sure there were no others, she would call aloud their names and at the end would shout :

" Are there any more, that I have missed ? "

When no answer came, Mary Ann would trip blithesomely back along the path, halt by the favoured one of the evening and say : " Come, Donald," or " 'Tis you to-night, Thomas," or " You look fine gay this eve, Willie," or " Wast waiting for me, David ? " She would give no heed to the others apart from the one she chose. The lucky one would leap down from the fence and he and Mary Ann Weatherup would go swinging away, hand in hand, in the evening time. The others disappeared, some abruptly, some lingeringly, to reappear the next night and perchance be chosen. Seldom, in such carnivals of choosing, was the same adorer selected on two successive evenings. Sometimes, a week or a fortnight, or even three weeks, passed before David, on the third section of the fence, was called, while Donald or Willie alternated for a week. Certain sections of the fence came to be regarded as lucky or unlucky, and significance attached also to the attitude of the sitter, as if crossed limbs or interlaced fingers could cast a magic spell upon the comely Mary Ann Weatherup.

Once or twice Mary Ann Weatherup hastened home and remained there in seclusion for a time. Later there were grandchildren but no son-in-law at the Weatherup family home. On the first occasion the Mother Weatherup grieved and reproached Mary Ann and admonished her not to let it happen again. On the second occasion she upbraided Mary Ann, and said she was imposing on the good nature of her parents and overtaxing the capacity of their home. Mary Ann went away again and all was serene once more.

" Some Frenchmen were cutting cordwood in the township of Hope, not far from the farm of the parents of Mary Ann Weatherup, in November 1879," says Murray. " Their dog was nosing in the brush and they saw him running along with something in his mouth. They followed the dog, thinking he had a woodchuck, and, as all French woodsmen at that time believed, woodchuck was a splendid cure for rheumatism. They hailed the dog and he dropped his burden. Instead of a woodchuck they found the body of a young child, roasted, partly devoured and frozen. They reported it to the authorities and I was notified. I went to the township of Hope.

"The fame of Mary Ann Weatherup was not abroad in that immediate part of the land so much as might have been supposed. I began a systematic search for the mother of the child. In due time I came upon Mary Ann Weatherup and arrested her. She denied the motherhood of any child within a year or more. When she was locked up her father and mother became frightened and disappeared. They had made sworn statements under examination before they ran away. I had Mary Ann kept in gaol and went to see her there. Finally she told me the story.

"'Maw was most unjust,' said Mary Ann. 'When I had my first child she used harsh words to me, and when I had my second child she accused me of imposing on her and paw, who had both hands full, said maw, with a family of their own. I went away and at length I went home again. "What again?" said Maw, as she looked at me, and she was most angry and charged me with trying to crowd her out of her own house. She called in paw, who swore I must get out. I sat down and folded my hands, and said : " Here I am and here I stay." They raged and stormed until I asked them what they thought I had them as my paw and maw for. They had not thought of this, for it silenced paw. He could see he owed me a duty. But maw she vowed she had done more than her duty by me when she let me grow into long dresses and put my hair up. Maw took after queer kind of people. She was not like paw. Paw could be subdued. I stayed despite maw. She kept vowing she would have a Judgment Day on earth and do some reckoning. On the day the boy was born maw stirred up a big fire in the stove. She almost melted us, and paw he went out to cool himself. The stove got red hot. Maw she came and grabbed the baby from me and laid him on the stove and roasted him, and then took him out and threw him in the woods. She said that would be a lesson to me not to try to overcrowd the house.'

"Mary Ann did not know where her parents had gone, when they ran away. At least she vowed she did not. One day a letter came addressed to her and postmarked away up in the Huron Peninsula. I got it and tried to decipher it, but it was beyond me and beyond any one else who tried to read it. Mary Ann said it was from her maw and had been written by her paw, and was intended to be an epistle of abuse, as the only other kind of letter her paw could write was one of praise, and his commendatory notes were less full of blots and splashes than his condemnatory communications.

"I went up to the wilds of Huron Peninsula and found Mary Ann's parents living in a remote, out-of-the-way place. It was easy to locate them approximately by the postmark on the letter, and then drive through the country until I found some one who knew of such a family. I brought them back and had them indicted for perjury. The mother was sent to gaol. They were ignorant people and very poor and ill-tutored. Mary Ann was kept in the common gaol for a year or so and then she was released. She went back to working out with farmers.

"Mary Ann never quite got over her coquettish ways. But her sojourn in gaol made her more thoughtful and her folks never thereafter had cause to complain of Mary Ann Weatherup trying to crowd them out of their own house."

14

THE CAPTURE OF LOCHINVAR SPROULE

THE paw and maw of Mary Ann Weatherup were still in hiding in the wilds of the Huron Peninsula when an elopement occurred in the county of Elgin. W. W. Sproule was the hero and a barber's wife from Aylmer was the heroine. Sproule was a spruce, sleek, dapper lover, and about forty years old, whose old home was in the maritime provinces, where his family was so influential that it was able to throw out a helping hand to its romantic offspring in the county of Elgin and have him appointed bailiff by the county judge without even the formality of giving security. Sproule's love affairs proved costly, and when he skipped by the light of the moon with the barber's wife, the judge found a double reason for desiring him to return.

"Sproule defaulted as bailiff," says Murray. "The barber of Aylmer was wroth and he missed his wife, for she was reputed to be a good housekeeper. The case came to me, and Sproule was wanted, both as an eloping defaulter and a defaulting eloper. I started for the maritime provinces, for it was dollars to doughnuts that the festive Lothario was back among his old-time friends. Sure enough he was at his old home in Hampton, about twenty miles from St. John's, after an absence of twenty-five years. I made a few preliminary inquiries and learned that his brother was the sheriff of the county, that another brother was deputy-sheriff, that another brother was a lawyer, that another brother was clerk of the court, that a nephew was a conductor on the road, that another nephew was a brakeman, and, truth to tell, almost every fifth man in that part of the country was a Sproule. I realised at the outset that strategy alone would enable me to land my man.

"I called on the old chief of police in the city of

St. John's and told him I would like to have an officer. I mentioned no names. I simply said I wanted to arrest a Canadian near Hampton. The people in the maritime provinces do not call themselves Canadians, but they call Canada the remainder of the Dominion. The chief informed me he had an officer who had come from that part of the country and would send him to me the next day. The next morning this detective called. Weatherhead was his name. It was March 1st, 1880. I told him, as we were about to start that my man was in Hampton. Weatherhead said all right and asked his name. I foolishly told Weatherhead Sproule's name. The detective immediately said he had to go to the office a minute. He went, too. I afterward learned that the chief of police and one of Sproule's brothers were personal friends, but I did not know it then. Weatherhead returned and we boarded a local train, mixed passenger and freight, and went to Hampton. At that time I had to get a warrant from one province indorsed in another, but since then all that has been changed. Weatherhead told me the only magistrate there was Mr. Barnes, registrar of the county. We hunted up Barnes. One of Sproule's brothers was his clerk. Weatherhead said again that Barnes was the sole magistrate within a radius of miles, and I reluctantly had to accept his word. Barnes was at the court house. He dilly-dallied and wasted time until I took a copy of the statutes and said :

"'There's the law, sir, and there's the warrant issued by the county judge, sign it or not!'

"He signed it after further delay. It was three miles from the court house to the town proper. Hampton was a little gut of a town, stretched along one street. Weatherhead said we could not get a rig to drive, and it was too far to walk, under the circumstances. Up to this time I had accepted Weatherhead in good faith. While I had my suspicions I was loth to believe that a fellow detective would betray me or sell me out. Never before had such a thing happened to me, and I am thankful to say that few times, in all the years of my experience, have I known one detective to play another false. I have found the men of the police business of the world honourable, fair and square in their dealings one with another, and the cases of sell-out have been the exceptions with me. But I was weary of Weatherhead.

"'I will go myself,' said I to him. 'I see through this pretty well.'"

"'Hold on,' said Weatherhead.

"'No, sir, I don't hold on,' said I. 'I go myself. Good day to you, sir.'

"I left him in the road, this Detective Weatherhead of St. John's. He followed me. I walked on to Hampton, and on the way I met a boy and gave him a quarter to show me where the returned Sproule was living in the little town. The boy piloted me to a double house and showed me the door and left me. I rapped. No one answered. I rapped at the next door and a lady answered my knock and said that Mr. and Mrs. Sproule left in a great hurry a few minutes before I arrived. They drove away with their trunks and a fast team, she said. I went back to the Sproule house and got in through a back door. I found the dishes on the table, the stove hot and other signs that the people had gone in a hurry. I had missed them by a mere few moments. I was satisfied then that I was sold. I was mad as a hornet, but I put a fair face on it and smiled.

"'I'm glad they're gone,' said I. 'I was not anxious to take them back, for it was not so serious a crime, after all. I had to go to Quebec and was ordered to stop here on the way.'

"I went back to my hotel at St. John's. The chief of police called to take me for a drive and to meet the men of the town. I declined. I saw the sheriff of St. John's, whom I had met before, and I told him of the Sproule matter in Hampton. I told all of them that I was going away, and desired them not to bother about Sproule. Outwardly I was smiling, but inwardly I was vexed and determined to take Sproule, of Hampton, back to the county of Elgin, no matter what games were played to block me.

"In St. John's, commercial travellers have to pay a licence to sell goods. Sometimes they leave their goods outside the city and take customers out to look at them. I told the clerk of the hotel to get me a good, lusty man, as I wanted to go to Sussex, twenty-five miles out, where I had some samples to bring in. The clerk got me a big Irish porter, who was not afraid of anything.

"'Bring two good lanterns and a stout stick,' said I to the porter. 'The scoundrels may steal my samples.'

"The spirit of adventure stirred the porter and he was eager for an encounter. We took the train for Hampton the next evening. The conductor smiled at me. The porter and I walked three miles to Sproule's in the darkness. I stationed him at the front door.

"'Grab anybody that comes out,' said I.

"I entered by the back door. I prowled through the entire house. The Sproules were not there. I left the house by the front door and as I stepped outside I was seized and whirled violently out into the road with a human hyena on top of me, yelling:

"'I've got ye! I've got ye!'

"It was my Irish porter obeying orders to seize any one coming out of the front door. He recognised me in a moment and promptly dusted me off and we went back to St. John's, empty-handed again.

"The next evening I boarded a train on which Sproules were part of the crew and doubled back to Moncton, one hundred and twenty miles. The Sproule brakeman followed me into the sleeper and made sure of my departure. I crept into my berth with my clothes on and drew the curtains. At Moncton I met the Halifax train going north. I slipped out of the sleeper, boarded the Halifax train and rode about fifty miles to Weldford, while the Sproule brakeman thought I was sleeping blissfully in my berth on the other train going to Quebec. At Weldford I stayed all night in a little hotel and then drove by stage, twenty-five miles away from the railroad, to Kingston, where I stayed a day and then drove to Rishabucto and stayed two days, and then I drove back to Weldford and thence by rail to Moncton, where I arrived on a storming, blowing night in March. The clerk at the American House, where I stopped, said they were out of liquor and cigars. I told him to go out and get a supply to last a few days. He went out and returned with two bottles of beer, two cigars, and a half-pint of whisky. It was too serious then to be as ludicrous as it seems to me now.

"A big storekeeper named McSweeny was president of the Moncton Council. I called at the store and met a Mr. McSweeny and told him the whole story from start to finish. He heard me through and said his brother was the Council president and that there was a bold, ambitious young fellow who wanted to become chief constable, and whose father was sheriff of the county and who knew the Sproules, of Hampton.

"'My brother has the appointment of the chief constable, and I think this man can help you,' said McSweeny.

"When President McSweeny came in he heard my story, and said: 'Murray, we'll see you do not go back without your man.' He sent for the candidate for chief constable. Vail was his name. McSweeny promised the appointment to him if he helped me get Sproule. I knew it was useless for me to try to run the gauntlet of Sproules, so I gave Vail some money and he went to Hampton while I waited in Moncton. He stayed with Sheriff Sproule in Hampton, and in a few days returned to Moncton empty-handed. His story was that my Sproule was still away, but would be home the next week. I gave no sign of incredulity and four days later I sent Vail to Hampton again, with the warrant endorsed and regular. The next day I received a telegram reading :

"'Got him!'

"I took the next train to Hampton. Sure enough, Sproule had returned and Vail had nabbed him. The Sheriff Sproule was enraged at his guest, Vail, who grinned and said he would be a chief constable soon. I started back with Sproule. The conductor of the train was the Conductor Sproule who had given me the laugh. I had the pleasure, this time, of a broad smile at him. I left the wife of the barber of Aylmer, in Hampton. I handcuffed Sproule. In travelling with a handcuffed prisoner you have to sleep side by side with him in the berth. Every time Sproule thought I was asleep in the berth he would yank me by jerking the arm by which he was handcuffed to me. I had to laugh. I really enjoyed his wrath. I took him back to St. Thomas and turned him over to the authorities in the county of Elgin.

"I never forgot the sell-out that was worked on me. Treachery is one of the rancid, nasty wrongs of life. Ingratitude is another. If in eternity there are figures before doorways to denote the character of the interiors, the Temple of Infamy will have its entrance flanked by a traitor and an ingrate. It is a source of pleasure to me that in matching my experience in my business with the experiences of other men in other businesses, I find that I have come into contact with far less treachery among my colleagues than they have encountered. It speaks well for the honour of men in the police business in so far as their dealings with one another are concerned. The Sproule case contained my first difficulty with an officer. I got my man just the same, and I often thought how much alike were the names of Mary Ann Weatherup, of Durham, and my friend, Detective Wetherhead, of St. John's, whom I left standing in the Hampton road."

15

BIG MAC OF SIMCOE, YOUNG SMITH, AND BILL NAY

A MIGHTY hunter lived in the county of Simcoe. His name was Henry McCormick. Everybody in those parts knew him as Big Mac. He was a giant, with the strength of two powerful men. He had been known to up-end a log as if it had been a barber's pole. He could shoulder a deer at noon and trudge till nightfall, with the burden on his back. At logging bees he led the gangs. In the early '70's in Canada some of the logging bees culminated in carnivals of fisticuffs and sometimes in revelries of death. After the big supper, when the day's work was done, whisky would be served like water and at last came murder in the moonlight. It was so in the case of Big Mac. At a logging bee in the county of Simcoe in 1870, with liquor flowing after the supper, a drunken row started, and a powerful fellow named John Pangman became involved with Big Mac. There was a brief struggle, then Big Mac stumbled on a stake from a sleigh. It was four feet long and very heavy. Big Mac seized it, thrust Pangman from him and smashed the stake down upon his head. Pangman went down in a heap, dead as a stone. Big Mac disappeared, taking with him his wife, who was at the logging bee.

Eleven years passed. The county of Simcoe was divided, the county of Dufferin being cut from it.

" After the new county were made," says Murray, " the old county's records were divided. The records of the townships in the new county went to the county of Dufferin. Included in them was the township of Mulmer in which Big Mac had killed Pangman in a drunken row. The new county had a new gaol, a new sheriff, and a new county Crown attorney, Mr. McMillan. He found this case of murder, eleven years old, and wanted to make business and communicated with the Department of Justice. I went to Orangeville, the county seat of the new county, and obtained full information of the crime and details of the life and appearance of Big Mac. The people all remembered him, a mighty man, a great hunter, a powerful fellow of colossal frame and tremendous strength, and one of the swiftest men afoot that the county ever had known. I obtained a perfect description of Big Mac as he had appeared eleven years before, and I billed him north, south, east, and west. No answer came. I found at last an old-time friend of Big Mac, who told me that Big Mac had travelled for several years after the murder and then had settled down near Saginaw in Michigan. I prepared extradition papers and then went to Saginaw.

"I located Big Mac near Coleman, Michigan. I got Officer Sutherland of Saginaw and went to Coleman. I knew that if Big Mac saw us first he would fight or flee. If he fought, it meant a desperate battle ; if he fled, it meant a long, hard chase. On July 15th, 1881, I arrived in Coleman. It was a hot day and I was wearing a blue serge suit. Sutherland and I went to Big Mac's house. No one was there. As we stood in the shade beyond the house I looked across the field and saw a man I knew at a glance was Big Mac. He was picking berries. He was indeed a giant. His wife was with him. We slipped down to the field beyond. A barbed wire fence was between. I hailed Big Mac and asked where some one lived. Sutherland was on the other side of the field. I started over the barbed wire fence when I hailed Big Mac, and in my haste to get over, my serge suit, trousers and coat, became hooked on the barbs. I jerked to get free and split my trousers from end to end and tore two long slits in my coat. I struggled and tore my trousers almost completely off. Big Mac laughed like a lion roaring and his wife pulled her sunbonnet close down over her head. I tied my slit coat around my waist by the sleeves, wearing it like an apron, and went over to where Big Mac was waiting.

"'Aren't you Henry McCormick?' I asked.

"'Yes, what of it?' said Big Mac, still laughing.

88

"'I'll have to arrest you and take you back to Canada,' said I.

"Mrs. Mac let out a howl of rage and tore her sunbonnet off.

"'You naked barbarian,' she cried, 'you'll never take him out of Michigan alive.'

"I thought she might mean to call me a naked barbwirean! She started at me, but Big Mac drew her back.

"'Silence be,' said Big Mac. ''Tis a case for men, not women.'

"I thought he meant a finish fight there, and I knew I had him with my revolver against his fists. But Big Mac thrust out his wrists for the handcuffs and was as docile as a child. We went to his house and I borrowed a pair of trousers, that looked on me as if an ostrich were to don the hide from an elephant's legs. Big Mac enjoyed my plight. I verily think it was the sight of me struggling on the fence, that put him in the good humour to submit tamely to arrest.

"I took him to Saginaw. He employed as counsel the Hon. Tim Tarsney, later a member of Congress, and a son of Judge Gage, before whom the extradition case was to be argued. I employed Mr. Durand, and I had seen Judge Gage about the case. Naturally I felt a little squeamish with a son of the judge against me. Big Mac had friends in Michigan and one of his sons had married and his friends had money. I swore a number of witnesses from Canada at the extradition hearing. Judge Gage was strictly honest and committed Big Mac for extradition. I arrived in Orangeville with Big Mac on August 26th. He was a fascinating old fellow. Men liked him. Although he had been away eleven years he had many warm friends. He was tried at the Fall Assizes in 1881 and was convicted of manslaughter. The jury brought in a strong recommendation for mercy and Big Mac was sentenced to one year in the county gaol.

"I remember one of the spectators at Big Mac's trial was an old man named John Smith, who had passed his seventieth birthday, yet farmed like a youngster and lived alone with a fifteen-year-old nephew, Johnnie, on his farm in the township of Amaranth, county of Dufferin. The old fellow was supposed to have money and to keep a snug sum hid in his house. On Saturday night, January 21st, 1882, while Big Mac was serving his year in gaol, fire partly burned the house of old man Smith. The nephew ran to a neighbour's house, cap in hand. He told the neighbour that as he sat with his uncle, two shots were fired through an uncurtained window. One pierced his cap, the other, he thought, struck his uncle, who fell. Flames broke out and the nephew ran for help.

"The neighbour, with others, went to the Smith farmhouse. It was partly burned. The old man was found on the floor, dead, with part of one leg burned off. The doctors laid the old man out and washed him. They found no marks of a wound on him and no trace of any bullet. I arrived in the night and the doctors reported no marks of a wound on the body. I got a lamp and went to the old man's house with the doctors. He had not been coffined, and I went over the body carefully. I finally discovered a punctured wound beneath the breast, so located and of such size as to pass almost unnoticed. In fact, the doctors had failed to observe it. I pointed it out. They examined it.

"'Is that an ante-mortem or post-mortem wound?' I asked.

"' Ante-mortem,' they agreed.

"We traced up the wound and found the bullet. It was such as would fit a thirty-two calibre revolver. I saw Mr. Hannah, the hardware merchant in Shelburne, the town nearest the Smith farmhouse, and I learned that young Smith, the nephew, had bought a thirty-two calibre Smith and Wesson revolver at his store shortly before the mysterious death of old man Smith. The revolver was not to be found. I searched the premises several times, and finally I began to drain the well. In its bottom I came upon the revolver and fished it out. Young Smith was arrested and held for trial. He was locked up in the county gaol at Orangeville, where Big Mac was serving his year for the murder of Pangman. The boy was close mouthed.

"I had been in Big Mac's good graces ever since I first met him in the berry patch in Michigan, with my trousers in shreds. I instructed Big Mac to find out what he could from the boy. Mac made friends with young Smith and promised to take him to Michigan, and eventually got the whole story of the crime from the boy. Young Smith was tried in October 1882. Big Mac was a witness against him. He went on the stand and told, under oath, the story as the boy had related it to him. George Galbraith was attorney for the boy and Aemelius Irving, Crown attorney, prosecuted. Galbraith gave Big Mac a severe cross-examination on the line that he was my detective. Some of the gaol officials swore they would not believe Big Mac under oath. The jury brought in a verdict acquitting young Smith, Later I took up the matter of the conduct of some of the gaol officials and attended to it.

" Big Mac returned to Michigan after serving his year. I kept the revolver for some time that young Smith bought shortly before his uncle was murdered. The bullet found in his uncle's body fitted the cartridge of the revolver. I regarded that as quite an interesting coincidence. But coincidences occasionally fail to convict.

" I recall one case, about the same time, that was full of more than coincidences. Yet the most powerful antidote to convincing evidence was present in the form of friends on the jury, and the result was acquittal. It was a crime that duplicated in marvellous accuracy of detail, the murder of old Abel McDonald by the Youngs. It occurred in 1881 and if it had been patterned after the McDonald tragedy it could not have fitted it more precisely.

" A team of horses with a waggon and no driver ran into a stump, on the road leading out of Barrie into the farming country of the county of Simcoe, and stopped. It was twilight on November 18th. A farmer saw the team standing there and climbed into the wagon and found an old man lying dead, with his head beaten in with an axe handle. The farmer recognised him as Thomas Sleight, an old fellow of sixty-six, who was a farmer in the township of West Guillembury. The team, when it stopped, was in the township of Innisfil, on the road leading to the township of Guillembury, so the crime became known as the Innisfil West tragedy. I took up the case.

" Sleight had driven from his farm to Barrie with a load

of cider and potatoes. He sold them and started home at sundown with the cash in his pocket. I skirmished the entire county for a clue to the perpetrator of the crime. I visited farmhouse after farmhouse, talking with all the inmates. Three or four persons were locked up and released after accounting for themselves. Finally, near the town of Bondhead, I got Bill Nay, about twenty-six years old, son of a farmer. Bill always was broke. The day after Sleight's murder Bill had money. I arrested him and searched him and found money on him, and Bill, at that time, was not clear as to where he got all of it. When the coroner's inquest was held, I had a strong case of circumstantial evidence against him. The inquest resulted in a verdict of murder against Bill and he was held for trial. I scoured the county for evidence. I found a little girl of fifteen, who saw Bill get into old man Sleight's waggon on the way out the Barrie road. I had other witnesses who saw him coming away along the road.

" Bill Nay was tried at Barrie at the Spring Assizes in 1882. He was defended by a great lawyer, an able man, the Hon. Dalton McCarthy, of Barrie, a Member of Parliament and a brilliant advocate. Colin McDougal, of St. Thomas, prosecuted. Judge Strong presided and charged the jury strongly against Bill Nay. There was quite a connection of Nay's in the county and Dalton McCarthy was a lawyer who knew the county thoroughly and a man who missed no opportunities in behalf of a client. The jury was out a long time. Bill Nay was on the anxious seat in great suspense. But the jury came in with an acquittal, and Bill Nay's friends reminded him that Dalton McCarthy was an able man and that friends on a jury were like pearls beyond price.

" An interesting coincidence of this case is that I heard Bill Nay was killed since. Big McCormick, young Smith, and Bill Nay were three vastly different individuals. The law dealt with each of them in its own way. Of the three, I like to think of Big Mac rather than of young Smith or, least of all, Bill Nay."

16

THE NEW YEAR'S MURDER OF STILLWELL OF BAYHAM

ONE-EYED Ranse Forbes was considered the best shot in his section of the county of Elgin. Ranse lived near Eden, in the township of Bayham. He had a sister, Jennie, and the two frequently visited at the home of Lewis N. Stillwell, a young farmer, who lived with his wife and two children in the same township of Bayham. Ranse and Mrs. Stillwell were old acquaintances, and Stillwell and Ranse's sister had known each other for a long time.

"On New Year's Day, 1885," says Murray, " Ranse and his sister Jennie, and Albert Thomas, the son of a neighbouring farmer, were at the Stillwells'. It was a jolly party. Stillwell was about thirty-five years old, Ranse was twenty-eight years old, and Thomas, the youngest of the three, was twenty-two years old. They had a fine dinner at the Stillwells' that day. A neighbour who asked for Stillwell that evening was told he had gone to his father's house. Forbes and Thomas told other neighbours that Stillwell had started on the afternoon of New Year's Day to visit his parents. The parents had seen nothing of him, so on the following Saturday a searching party was organised, and fields and woods were beaten, and the body of Stillwell was found in a clump of woods some distance from his house. He was dead.

" A bullet hole in the back of the head and a hole in the forehead showed how he had died. I went to the place. The shot had been a beauty. It required a perfect marksman to put a bullet in the head so it would bore, as it came out, a hole directly through the centre of the forehead. I learned that Ranse had borrowed a forty-four calibre Spencer repeating rifle on December 26th from a man named Rutherford. I learned also by thorough inquiry that Forbes had bought a box of forty-four calibre cartridges at Golding's. I questioned young

Thomas. He was not communicative. In fact, after I had left him he said to a friend, 'The authorities will have to stretch my neck as long as a fence rail before I'll squeal."

"No one had even suggested squealing or confessing to this young man, so far as I knew. But I promptly heard what he had said, and it decided me finally as to my course in the case. I learned from the women at the Stillwell house on New Year's Day that after dinner on that day Stillwell, Forbes, and Thomas went down to the clump of woods in which Stillwell's body was found. I learned also that along towards twilight Forbes and Thomas returned to the Stillwell house alone. They were committed for trial.

"Soon after they were committed, a magistrate of the neighbourhood came to me, and asked if Thomas could tell the whole truth. Thomas's father and sister had called on him. I saw Judge Hughes, and Thomas was called in before Forbes and Mrs. Stillwell, and he, the young man whose neck would be stretched as long as a fence rail before he would squeal, voluntarily confessed, and told his story of what had happened. He said that after the three entered the woods, Forbes walking behind, shot Stillwell in the back of the head, the bullet passing out through the forehead. Forbes and Thomas then returned to the house, leaving Stillwell dead in the woods. When they arrived at the house, said Thomas, Forbes said to Mrs. Stillwell, 'Come back to the kitchen.' When she went to the kitchen, said Thomas, Forbes told her, 'We've done the job.'

"The trial was held at the Spring Assizes. Judge Matthew Cruiks Cameron, of whose extensive career as a defender of prisoners I already have spoken, presided at the trial, as he had become a judge some years before. McDougal and Robertson were counsel for the accused, and Colter, of Cayuga, prosecuted. The defence, of course, knew that young Thomas was to testify against Forbes. They set out to nullify his testimony. They got some one into the gaol who talked that Forbes was going on the stand and swear that it was Thomas, not he, who did the shooting. When Thomas was on the witness-stand at the trial, he was asked in cross-examination if he had heard any one say that Forbes had stated he would swear Thomas did the shooting? Thomas replied that he had heard such talk.

"'Who was doing the talking, did you think?' he was asked.

"'I thought detectives were those talking it,' he answered.

"Judge Cameron discarded his evidence. The defence made an able fight, and the verdict was acquittal.

"I was in California on another case at the time of the trial, and was not present during any part of it. The case was one of interest at the time, for the public seemed to have well-defined ideas as to how the death of Stillwell had occurred. Confessions are not always effective, even if they should happen to be true in every detail. The circumstances surrounding every episode of significance in a case are certain to weigh heavily one way or the other. I have seen direct evidence, given under unfavourable circumstances, thrown out or rendered ineffective by reason of these very disadvantages of circumstances. Circumstantial evidence is harder to upset than direct evidence in certain respects. A positive fact, relying on a direct statement for its confirmation, may fail by reason of the statement being involved in extraneous matters damaging to its own good repute or validity. A positive fact, borne out by circumstances, needs no further confirmation.

"The Stillwell case demonstrated clearly that some one was lying desperately. Thomas said Forbes shot Stillwell. Thomas's statement was discounted because some one had stated Forbes said Thomas shot Stillwell. The accident theory, that Stillwell had shot himself, did not figure in the case. But the chief interest of the case, to my mind, was not in its mystery, for after the evidence was collected there was no mystery about it, but in the clever evasion of the effects of a damaging confession. And after all, young Thomas's neck was not stretched as long as a fence rail.

"The results of such a trial are permanent, even where there is an acquittal. For instance, in the township of Bayham, the entire countryside does not puzzle still as to who killed Stillwell. The trial served some good ends. The verdict was 'Not guilty.' The people heard it, and went on about their business. That was the only thing to do.

"Jennie Forbes, Ranse's sister, afterwards married the turnkey of the St. Thomas gaol."

THE WINTER ROAD TO MANITOULIN

ONE of the exciting times in the history of the Provincial Parliament was in 1885. It began in accusations of bribery and grew into a dynamite scare, in which some nervous members believed, as they sat in their seats, that the next minute they might be sailing skyward in fragments, along with the remnants of the building, all blown to pieces by a dynamite explosion.

"A plot or conspiracy had been hatched," says Murray, "to defeat the Mowat Government. Several cash offers were made, and it was stated that in certain instances money actually had been paid over to members to draw them away from the Government side. The Government got on to it, and there was great excitement in the House. Feeling ran high. There was bitterness on both sides.

"On top of all the excitement came the discovery that dynamite was placed round the building, and there was talk of a terrific explosion that was planned. At that time the old Parliament Building at Wellington and Front Streets was in use. There was a great scare over the dynamite affair, and the excitement grew. It culminated when some of the members arose and stated the amount of purchase money that had been offered to them to vote for the Opposition. Warrants were issued for the arrest of parties alleged to have tried to bribe members. Big Push Wilkinson, a politician, and others were arrested.

"One of the members, R. A. Lyon, living on Manitoulin Island, was absent at his home, and I was instructed to serve papers on him. It was in March 1885. Lyon lived far to the north, several hundred miles from Toronto. The time was limited. I went by rail to the end of the road at that time, Gravenhurst. I arrived in Gravenhurst on Tuesday,

March 3rd. A blizzard was raging. I hired a pair of horses and a sleigh, and struck out for the north, heading first for Sufferin, forty-five miles away. I had been over the road only once before, in the summer. I tried to hire a man to go with me, but none was willing to go. The snow was whirling and blowing and drifting, and the trail was hid, for long distances, beneath stretches of snow that rose and curved away like sand dunes. Night fell shortly after I started, and I pressed on in the dark hoping for a brighter moon. I had stuck in a drift a few miles out of Gravenhurst, and had found a rail fence near by. I appropriated one of the rails, and took it with me in the sleigh.

"About midnight I suddenly came upon the end of my road in a dense wood and a deep drift. The horses were stuck, the sleigh was fast. No house was in sight. I could move neither forward nor back. The snow drifted up against the sleigh. I seemed to have come into a pocket where the road ended. I tumbled out and floundered around. I had missed the main road and gone up a blind timber trail, and had driven into a drift. I got my fence rail and laboriously broke a road. Then I unhitched the horses, and tied them to a tree beside the sleigh. Then I tried to get the sleigh turned around. I dug the snow away from it with the rail, and finally got underneath it and lifted it around. In doing so, I stuck feet first in the snow underneath the sleigh. I struggled to get out, but was caught as if in a vice. The rail lay just beyond my reach. The wind was whirling the snow about me, and I was yearning for it to subside. I grimly calculated my chances of escape. I was up a blind trail, untravelled and abandoned. I could expect no help from passers-by, because there were no passers-by on such a road. As I thought it over, I was dealt a stinging blow across the face. It seemed to come from nowhere, yet I felt the burn of the welt. I began to dig with my hands to free my body from the drift, when a second smashing slash in the face made me turn in time to see the reins from the horses fly past in the wind. I waited, watching them. They whirled up again, and came swishing down. I grabbed and caught them. Then I began to pull and call to the horses to back up. They plunged a bit, then drew back, snapping the hitching

97

strap that tied them to the tree. I drew them over close by me, and fastened the reins through the traces and then wrapped them around me. Then I shouted to the horses and pelted them with snowballs, and wriggled and kicked as best I could. They leaped forward, and at last I felt myself coming up out of the drift.

" I hitched the team to the sleigh again, and beat my way back along the timber trail to the main trail, and pressed on. It was a rough, hilly, rocky country. The wind was howling and tearing at the trees in the forest. I remembered that Sufferin simply was a farmhouse with a barn and a big tree— a giant, standing alone near the barn. Every big tree that loomed up caused me to stop and alight and stumble through the snow in search of a house or barn. At half-past one in the morning I heard a long, loud howl. I stopped and listened. It sounded again, ahead of me. I drove forward, listening, and saw in the night another big tree. I alighted, and started toward it, and a dog rushed through the drifts to me. I followed him, and found the farmhouse of Sufferin. I went back for my team, brought them up, and hailed the house. A woman answered ; the man was ill. I stabled the horses. They were too hot to feed, and I had to wait up with them until three o'clock. It was biting cold. I took the buffalo robes into the house, and laid down on the floor by the stove at three o'clock, and slept two hours.

"At half-past five o'clock in the morning I started for Parry Sound, thirty miles from Sufferin. It was afternoon when my tired team dragged its weary way into Parry Sound, The horses were exhausted. I stabled them, and called on Postmaster Ainsley and Judge McCurry, the stipendiary magistrate. I had over one hundred and fifty miles by the nearest route from there to Manitoulin Island. I searched Parry Sound for a man to go. None would make the trip. It was a wild route over a desolate way. There was no road, no trail. There were stretches of ice that ended suddenly in open water, there were rocky trails along bits of land, there were yawning cracks in ice and deep chasms in snow. Some had to be bridged with trees, others had to be circled for miles around. They said no team could make the trip, that only a dog sled could hope to get through in such weather. I finally found a fellow named Elliott who agreed to go, naming his own price. He had been a sailor and hunter and trapper and fisherman, and knew the whole country. After agreeing to go, he went out and came back shortly, and declined to go.

"'Name your own price,' said I.

"He gave me a raise on his first figure, and agreed to go. He went out, came back, and declined again.

"'For the third and last time, name your own price,' said I.

"Elliott gave me another raise, saying there were some bad holes in the ice that he had not remembered at first. He went out again, and came back and said he would have to buy some new snow shoes or he could not go. I bought them for him. He went out and came back and said he would have to buy a new dog sled or he could not go. I bought a new dog sled for him. He went out, and back he came again and said he had to buy another dog or he could not go. I bought the new dog for him. He came back for two extra blankets. I bought them.

"'And here are three bottles of brandy,' I said. 'Now will you go?'

"'It's a go this time,' said Elliott.

"He brought up his sled and four dogs, and I gave him the papers and conduct money. To make sure he would go, I drove ten or twelve miles with him on the ice of Georgian Bay, as far as I could go. Then I had to turn back to Parry Sound, as I could go no farther. I saw him go singing over the ice with his dogs. He had chosen a route of two hundred and seventy miles. He slept out with his dogs on the way. He made his way through, too ; thanks, I suppose, to the brandy, from his point of view. Lyon was served with the papers. I made my way back to Toronto, driving to Gravenhurst by daylight from Sufferin.

"The bribery cases dwindled to nothing, like all bribery investigations, as a rule. No one was sent to prison. No dynamite exploded. All grew tranquil, and the Mowat Government was not upset. On the road to Sufferin was the only time in my life when I was grateful for a slap in the face, repeated on one cheek and the other also."

18

THE LONG POINT MYSTERY

THE lighthouse keeper on Long Point, on the north shore of Lake Erie, near Port Rowan, was sitting by the window one bitter cold morning in December 1884. The waves were pounding shoreward over a fringe of ice. The wind was howling in a gale, and not a sign of life was visible over the expanse of waters. The keeper idly swept the shoreline with his gaze, from horizon on the right to horizon on the left. He saw nothing but tumbling waters and icy rime. He poked the fire and resumed his seat. As he glanced out he saw a black object bobbing in the water; it rose and fell and rolled as the waves beat in or receded; it was coming shorewards. Thrice it was tossed up on the ice, and thrice it glided back and slid with a splash into the water. The fourth time the waters seemed to lift it up and toss it forward so that it lay a shapeless bundle on the shore.

The keeper of the light levelled his glasses on it, and instantly laid them aside, donned his cap and coat, and hurried out. He ran down the shore to where the object lay, and knelt beside it. The figure was that of a man. The body was wound with rope, and the limbs were rope-bound. The hands were tied. Dickinson, the light keeper, picked up the icy body and carried it to the lonely lighthouse. He judged it was a sailor from some vessel of the lakes, gone to a watery grave and cast ashore long after death. He made a rough box, cut away the ropes from the body, and buried it as it was, boots and all, on Long Point. He marked the grave of the unknown dead with a board; there was no clue to the man's identity. His features were the face of a stranger; he wore no hat, his clothing was unmarked. Snow soon hid the grave, and Dickinson forgot about it, save for an occasional wondering, as he sat by the fire in the long

100

winter nights, whether the man had come to his death by fair means or foul; whether he had died in his bunk naturally or whether in the night he had been seized and bound and buried alive in the waters that may give up their dead but tell no tales of their tragedies. A paragraph in the newspapers some days later said simply that an unknown body had been washed ashore on Long Point and had been buried by the keeper of the lighthouse.

"Three months later," says Murray, "John Piggott, of Bay City, Michigan, communicated with the Government about this body. For months John Piggott had been searching for his brother Marshall Piggott. Marshall was a young farmer, twenty-nine years old, who lived in the township of Malahyde, county of Elgin, Ontario, about forty miles from Port Rowan. His father, before he died, gave him a small farm of about fifty acres on the shore of Lake Erie. Piggott married Sarah Beacham, a neighbouring farmer's daughter, and they settled on the little farm. They had no children. In the early part of 1884 Sarah died mysteriously, and one of the features of her death was a violent attack of retching. Marshall Piggott was not a bright man, but rather slow and simple minded. At ten o'clock on the morning of November 17th, 1884, a few months after his wife died, Marshall was seen going down the road toward the lake near his house. That was the last known of him. Some of the neighbours, when he failed to appear, thought he had gone on a visit to his brother John in Michigan. When John heard of it he began a search for his brother. He read the newspapers carefully for tidings of unknown dead, and when the Long Point burial was printed he saw it, and once more communicated with the Government. This was in March 1885, and on March 10th I went to St. Thomas and met John Piggott, and conferred with Judge Hughes.

"John Piggott and I then went by train to Aylmer and thence drove to Port Rowan, and then drove on the ice to Long Point. We had the body dug up and the coffin opened. The body was decomposed, but John Piggott identified it positively as the body of his brother Marshall Piggott. He identified the boots as a pair he had worn and had given to Marshall. He identified a peculiar mark on the big toe of the right foot, and he also identified the peculiar pigeon-breast. William Dickinson, the lighthouse keeper, said that the face, when he found the body, bore a strong resemblance to the face of John Piggott. He said John and the dead man looked alike. There was little face when we saw the body; the head had been smashed in and the chin broken. Satisfied that the body was that of Marshall Piggott we had it taken to Port Rowan and buried. On March 24th I drove the mother of Marshall Piggott from her home in Nilestown, county of Middlesex, to Port Rowan and had the body exhumed, and the mother identified the clothes and the body.

"Who killed him? The question presented itself the moment I saw the crushed skull and the lighthouse keeper told me of the way the body was bound with rope, and the way the hands and limbs were tied. It was not suicide. The rope and the wounds settled that; no man could have tied himself in such a manner. I asked the mother when she first heard of her son going away. She said that the day after Marshall disappeared in November, Havelock Smith, a young man, twenty-eight years old, who lived with his widowed mother on her farm, near the farm of Marshall Piggott, and whose family was respected highly and prominent in the country, had appeared at the house and said he wanted to see her alone. Her son, young William Piggott, was with her that day, making ready to go to Oregon to live. William stepped outside, and Havelock Smith then showed her a note for $1,300 made to him, ostensibly by Marshall Piggott. Havelock Smith told her, said the mother, that Marshall had given him the note the day before in exchange for $1,300, and Marshall had said he was going away. The note was dated the day Marshall disappeared. When asked where he got the money to lend to Marshall Havelock Smith said he borrowed it from Richard Chute. Mrs. Piggott said she would have to find her son, Marshall, before she could do anything about the note. She called her son young William, and told him to go to Marshall's place and look after it. I saw William. He told me he had driven back from Nilestown to Marshall's with Havelock Smith, and on the way Havelock asked William to help him get the money. The story about borrowing the money from Richard Chute I found untrue.

"I went to Marshall's place, and I looked Havelock Smith over. Then I visited the neighbours one by one. I learned from Walter Chute and from Mrs. John Hankenson that on the day Marshall disappeared Havelock Smith went to Piggott's house about half-past nine o'clock in the morning. Smith and Piggott were seen later walking away in a south-easterly direction, toward Smith's farm. That was the last seen of Piggott alive. I learned that about four o'clock that afternoon Smith was seen by Walter Chute and his son, Ensley Chute. Smith had been seen first going toward a gully about half a mile from Piggott's house, and he was seen later coming back from the gully. This gully led to the lake, and was secluded. Walter Chute spoke to Smith on his way back; Smith's trousers were wet, as if he had been in the water. A shot had been fired while Smith was in the gully. Smith told Chute he had shot at a grey fox and missed it.

"I learned that on the Sunday before Piggott disappeared Smith went to Port Royal, six miles away, and hired a row boat, and took it to his own gully and left it there the day Piggott disappeared.

"I began a search for the weapon. I learned that some years before part of an old steamer had drifted ashore, and in the wreckage were some iron grate bars, each weighing about one hundred pounds. Walter Chute had found these bars, He had a maple sugar bush near the gully, and for arches in his sugar-boiling furnaces he used some of these grate bars. Shortly after Piggott disappeared Chute was in his maple grove and he missed one of these bars.

"The theory of the prosecution was that Piggott had been inveigled to the gully to help launch the boat, that while launching the boat he was struck with a heavy, blunt instrument, which smashed his skull and drove his head down so that the chin was broken on the gunwale of the boat, that the iron bar was taken out in the boat, and tied to the body which was dropped in deep water. After the body was in the water some time it wanted to rise. The motion of the water, washing the body to and fro, cut the rope, the body rose and drifted forty miles to Long Point, near Port Rowan, where the lighthouse keeper found and buried it. This theory was upheld by the wounds on the head, the skull being smashed and the chin fractured. The shot heard by the Chutes was believed by the prosecution to be a blind to account for Smith's presence in that vicinity, as if hunting for a grey fox. The rope was not a new rope. I searched the country for miles around, but could get no trace of where it was obtained. It was not an uncommon kind of rope.

"We got a tug and dragged the lake in the vicinity. We found the bar, and a piece of rope, and Piggott's hat. The hat was anchored to a stone. I learned also that after Piggott disappeared, Smith went to Buffalo, and on his return he said he had heard from Piggott while in Buffalo.

"Havelock Smith was arrested on Tuesday, March 24th. Arthur Belford, a friend of Smith, also was arrested, but later was discharged. The preliminary investigation was quite lengthy. Smith was remanded for trial. Young William Piggott had gone to Oregon to live, and I went out to Portland, and brought him back on April 28th, and he gave evidence against Smith.

"The trial of Havelock Smith began on Tuesday, November 24th, 1885, at St. Thomas. Chief Justice Armour presided. It became a famous case. John Idington, of Stratford, prosecuted for the Crown, assisted by Donald Guthrie, of Guelph, and County Attorney James Coyne, now registrar of the county of Elgin. Colin McDougal, James Robertson, and Edward Meredith defended Smith. The prosecution swore 108 witnesses. The defence swore a large number. The defence maintained that the body found by Dickinson, the lighthouse keeper, was not the body of Piggott. A Dr. McLay had obtained an order from the coroner, and had exhumed the body, and said that no one could tell whether it was the body of a white person or black person, man or woman. Aaron Dolby testified that Dr. McLay told Mrs. Dolby there was no doubt it was Piggott's body. The defence also put in an alibi with Smith's mother as the chief witness. An excerpt from the report of the charge of Chief Justice Armour to the jury will give a good idea of the trend of the testimony. The Chief Justice said, in part:

"'The prisoner (Smith) had a motive and interest in removing Marshall Piggott. Had any other person an interest or motive? If you believe that the body is that of Marshall Piggot and the note is a forgery, which could not be realised on except by the removal of the maker, then does not the evidence point conclusively to the prisoner as the perpetrator of the crimes? Why did the prisoner make so many untrue statements? What was the object of prisoner's visit to Buffalo? He told several people he had received a letter from Marshall at Buffalo. Why wasn't the letter produced? Wasn't the whole thing a blind to throw suspicion off himself? Who was it had the opportunity to kill Marshall, who had the motive, and who had the object? If you have reasonable doubt as to the guilt of the prisoner, then it is your duty to acquit him. But this doubt must be a reasonable one, gentlemen. If, after sifting the evidence thoroughly, and eliminating all that you believe to be false, you think that the evidence is equally divided as to the guilt or the innocence of the prisoner, then it is your duty to acquit him. But, if on the other hand, the facts and circumstances advanced by the Crown and the deductions to be drawn therefrom are, in your opinion, sufficiently strong to prove to you that Marshall Piggott met his death at the hands of an assassin, and that the prisoner was an active or passive participant in encompassing his death, then it is equally your duty to fearlessly and manfully record your verdict of guilty. You may now retire.'

"'The jury deadlocked. It stood five for conviction and seven for acquittal, and could not agree.

"The second trial was set for May 1886. The defence was not ready, and the trial went over until September 1886, before Judge O'Connor, at St. Thomas. The case was fought out again. In selecting the jury for this second trial I objected strongly to certain jurors, but the Crown attorneys overruled me. They said they were satisfied the jurors were all right. They thought the defence would object to some of them. I said the defence would not object, and it then would be too late for the Crown. The panel was almost exhausted, and, against my urgent advice, they accepted two of these jurors. The result showed the jurors I objected to were the mainstay in holding out for a disagreement. The jury at this second trial stood seven for conviction and five for acquittal. The prisoner was released on $8,000 bonds. I advised a third trial, as there was no question in my mind as to who did it. Smith had a number of influential friends. His brothers, Harvey and William, were highly esteemed. William was a member of the County Council. At both trials there was great sympathy for Havelock Smith's family and relatives.

"In this case the Chief Justice said to the jury: 'The only certainty that human affairs permits of is a high degree of probability. You are not expected to have direct evidence of a crime. If such were the law, ninety-nine out of one hundred guilty men would go unpunished. Criminals seek secrecy for their crimes. If a witness comes forward and says he saw a man kill another by a blow, or in any other way, there is always the possibility that he may be telling an untruth, and there must always be corroborative evidence of a circumstantial character.' The Chief Justice's charge, in the report, also contains the sentence: 'Circumstantial evidence is the best kind of evidence.'

"I read a lot of praise of the circumstantial case of the Crown against Havelock Smith. My mind is undimmed by a doubt on this case. Smith, the last I heard, still was around in that vicinity, and Marshall Piggott lies buried not far away."

19

JOHN STONE, GENTLEMAN

JOHN STONE was a cynic, an atheist, and an English gentleman. He came of an ancient and honourable family. His father educated him for the Church of England and his mother's heart's desire was to see him a clergyman. He graduated from Harrow (preparatory school only) and was famed among his classmen for his brilliancy. Instead of training for the pulpit he developed a yearning for the stage and he turned his back on the ministerial career planned by his parents, and devoted himself to the study of Shakespeare and the portrayal of Shakespearean rôles. He married a Miss Morley, a relative of the Right Hon. John Morley, and after loitering for a year or two he suddenly packed his trunks and sailed, with his wife, for America.

"He settled in Texas," says Murray, "and bought a large ranch not far from Dallas. Subsequently he moved into Dallas and was elected Mayor of Dallas and was re-elected. He was such a remarkable man, with such a command of language, that it is not strange he should become involved as the central figure in an affair which drew the attention of the President of the United States, the British Ambassador, the Attorney-General of the United States, and high officials of both Canada and the neighbouring country.

"Stone had a sister, a Mrs. Asa Hodge, who came from England to Canada and lived in Beamsville, county of Lincoln, twenty miles from Suspension Bridge. Her husband was a fruit grower. Mayor Stone of Dallas made occasional visits to New York, and on one of these trips he called to see his sister. One of her children, Maud Hodge was a beautiful girl of sixteen at this time. John Stone when he saw her liked her so much that he took her back

107

to Texas and kept her in his own family, educating her with his own children. Several years later Mrs. Hodge went to Texas to visit her brother and daughter. She did not like the look of things. Maude had grown to a lovely young woman of nineteen, and John Stone regarded her with jealous affection. Mrs. Hodge took her daughter away from Stone and brought her home to Beamsville, very much against Stone's wishes.

"John Stone tarried in Texas for a short time, and then he, too, went to Beamsville, where Maude was living. He started a cheese factory, and moved his family from Dallas to Beamsville. Maude Hodge became his clerk in the factory. At that time Stone was a man about forty-five years old, of remarkable personality and amazing command of language. He was a man of refined appearance, with sandy-brown hair and grey eyes, and rather classic features. One of his chief pleasures was to inveigh against churches and clergymen, and to mock at the calling for which he had been educated. He proclaimed himself an atheist, a believer in no church and in no creed. He denounced Christians as pretenders and the Christian life as a delusion and a sham. Consequently, when Maude, his favourite, became acquainted with Miss Chapman, a very fine lady and sister of the Rev. I. M. Chapman, pastor of the Baptist church of Beamsville, John Stone was displeased greatly. As Miss Chapman's influence over Maude grew, the young girl began to weary of her uncle's employ and went to the factory reluctantly. At length, in January 1886, she stayed away from the factory, remaining at her own home with her mother. John Stone waited in vain for her return. On January 5th he went to her house. Maude and her mother were sitting in the kitchen, chatting, about two o'clock in the afternoon, when Stone walked in.

"'Is Asa in?' he asked Mrs. Hodge.

"Asa was out. Mrs. Hodge said he would return presently. John Stone stepped over to Maude, opened his coat, drew something from an inside pocket and held it out to Maude.

"'Well, Maude, I guess you and I will close issues,' he said, as he opened his coat.

"The girl saw him draw forth the revolver and offer it to her. She shrank back.

"'Maude, shoot me,' said John Stone, holding out the revolver to her.

"Mrs. Hodge screamed and begged her brother not to shoot. Stone, without a word, fired three shots at his favourite. Mrs. Hodge ran out of the house shrieking. As she ran she heard a fourth shot, John Stone had walked to the door, put the pistol to his head and shot himself. Mrs. Hodge and several of the neighbours hurried to the house. Maude staggered out of the door and fell in the yard. She was carried to the house of a neighbour, Mrs. Konkle, and Drs. Jessop and McLean attended her, locating one bullet in the left side below the heart and another near the left shoulder blade. Stone was taken to his own home. The doctors thought both would die. Two constables were set to guard Stone at his own house, night and day. He hovered on the verge of death for five weeks, and suddenly, to everybody's surprise, he began to recover. Toward the middle of February the doctors said he soon could be removed to St. Catherine's gaol.

"I talked with him at that time and he impressed me as one of the most fluent talkers I ever had heard. Words flowed in a ceaseless, unbroken stream. His vocabulary was remarkable.

"'It was a high ambition ; these things cannot always be accounted for,' he said, referring to the shooting.

"In February a stranger, giving the name of Mr. Matthews, arrived in Beamsville. No one knew who he was or whence he came. He disappeared as suddenly as he had appeared. John Stone also disappeared. This was on February 14th. One of the constables guarding him possibly was not so much surprised as some others over his escape. I went to Beamsville and traced Stone, where he had driven in a carriage to Suspension Bridge and had crossed to the States and had taken a train. There I lost him. I returned to Beamsville and learned that Mr. Matthews had a satchel with him marked 'H.W.M., Balto.' I prepared extradition papers and went to Baltimore and found that Hugh W. Matthews, a rich

109

manufacturer, lived in a fine mansion at No. 263, West Lanvale Street, and was a prominent business man of high standing, in that city. On inquiry I ascertained that he was a brother-in-law of John Stone. It was March 5th when I arrived in Baltimore and I called on Chief Jacob Frey, an old friend. He detailed Detective Albert Galt to assist me. On March 6th Galt and I went to the Matthews's house and walked in and found John Stone lying on a lounge in the library gazing idly at the ceiling. I had laid an information before United States Commissioner Rogers, and Galt arrested Stone.

"In a twinkling the whole household, servants and all, were around us saying John Stone was ill and we could not take him. Dr. Bacon and Dr. Harvey hurried in, summoned by a member of the household, and told us we must not lay a hand on John Stone, as it would endanger his life. Discretion was the better part of valour. Stone had seemed quite comfortable when we entered, but he seemed to sink rapidly in five minutes. It may have been due to his earlier love for the stage and acting. I was satisfied he was shamming, and I left Galt with him in case he tried to escape again. I went back to Police Headquarters and saw Chief Frey and told him what had happened.

"'All right,' said Frey. 'If there he's ill, there he stays.'

"Frey detailed two more detectives, Tom Barringer and Mark Hagen, to join Galt. The three detectives arranged their tours of duty in shifts of eight hours, and they watched John Stone, keeping him in actual sight day and night.

"I called on Commissioner Rogers and on United States Marshal John McClintock. They said they could do nothing. I went to Washington and called on Sir Sackville West, then British Ambassador, and stated my case. Sir Sackville West called a carriage and drove me to the State Department. Thomas F. Bayard was Secretary of State. He was deaf as a post. We shouted the case to Mr. Bayard. He said he did not know what he could do until the case came into court. I returned to the British Legation with Sir Sackville, who was a very nice little gentleman. He advised me to get an American lawyer. He also gave me a letter to Dennis O'Donohue, at Baltimore, one of the oldest British Consuls on the continent. After leaving Sir Sackville I went to call on my old friend Senator Daniel W. Voorhees, of Indiana, who had been my counsel before in various extradition cases including the Meagher case in Indianapolis. He was living at The Portland and was indisposed, but he sent word for me to come right up.

" Three justices of the United States Supreme Court were calling on Senator Voorhees at the time. They were Justice Gray, Justice Field, and another. It was March 22nd. Voorhees made me blush telling the judges of old cases and heaping flattery on me.

" ' What is it this time, Murray?' he asked. ' Out with it. These gentlemen have heard cases stated before now— desperate cases, too, and desperately stated.'

" I told the case right then and there, the whole story, while the four men, three justices of the United States Supreme Court and Senator Voorhees listened.

" ' Is he dying?' they asked.

" ' I think he is feigning,' said I.

" ' Suppose he pleads insanity?' said one of the justices.

" ' It would not be upheld,' said I.

" ' But if the Commissioner decided against you?' he asked.

" ' Murray would appeal, so beware, gentlemen, beware,' said Senator Voorhees.

" The three justices departed, and I asked Senator Voorhees to take the case. He said he could not.

" ' But as an old friend I'll assist you in every way,' he said.

" I explained to him that Stone, through his rich brother-in-law, had retained William Pinckney White (former Governor of Maryland), ex-Judge Garey, W. M. Simpson, and Governor White's son, four able lawyers and influential men, to fight his case for him. Voorhees instantly told me not to be anxious, but to call the next morning and we would go to the Department of Justice. I did so, and Senator Voorhees and I called on Attorney-General A. H. Garland.

" ' Mr. Murray is a particular friend of mine, an officer of

111

Canada, who has come here after a refugee from justice named John Stone,' said Senator Voorhees.

"The Attorney-General questioned me, and I told him I was morally certain Stone was feigning. Mr. Garland dictated a letter to Marshal McClintock in Baltimore, and suggested a commission of United States surgeons be appointed to go to Baltimore and examine Stone, and see if he could be removed with safety. The letter of the Attorney-General of the United States to Marshal McClintock read :

'DEPARTMENT OF JUSTICE,
'WASHINGTON, March 23rd, 1886.

' 1999-1886.
JOHN MCCLINTOCK, Esq.,
  ' United States Marshal,
    'Baltimore, Md.
' SIR,

' It has been brought to my attention that John Stone is under arrest on an application by the Canadian authorities for extradition, and fears are entertained that Stone may make his escape, and avoid the investigation necessary to his extradition. I hope you will see to it, and take every precaution to that end, that he is safely kept until that examination is had. You will spare no pains to effect this.

' I am more particular in this matter than ordinarily, because last summer, on an application by this Government to the Canadian authorities for the extradition of an offender against our laws, every facility was afforded us and everything done by those authorities to enable us to bring back the offender, which we did, and I cannot afford to put this Government into the attitude of lacking in the proper comity towards those people. If any additional expense is necessary to secure this man's attendance, it will be paid by this Department.

' I have written to the Treasury Department that they request Surgeon Meade to make the examination which you desire.

'Very respectfully,
'A. H. GARLAND,
'Attorney-General.'

" Two United States surgeons proceeded to Baltimore after our call on the Attorney-General. I went on the same train. They drove to the Matthews' house. There they were joined by the family physicians, Dr. Bacon and Dr. Harvey, and two or three others. The civilian doctors already were in favour of the prisoner, for Stone was a prisoner in the Matthews' mansion. After the examination, the opinion of all the surgeons was that the removal of the prisoner would be dangerous, and any undue excitement might cause a rush of blood to the head and rupture a blood vessel, causing death instantly. The two United States surgeons returned to Washington and made a report to this effect. I also returned to Washington and saw Voorhees, and induced him to take the case. We called on Attorney-General Garland again, and saw him and his first assistant, Heber May, of Indiana, a friend of Senator Voorhees. Then Senator Voorhees and I went to Baltimore, and the three detectives who were watching Stone night and day told Senator Voorhees that Stone was feigning.

" Senator Voorhees, as counsel, had a writ of show cause issued on Marshal McClintock to learn why he could not produce John Stone in Court before Commissioner Rogers. The Marshal appeared with the affidavits of the doctors that Stone could not be moved. Matters went on, the three detectives keeping John Stone in sight every minute of the time. Sir Sackville West sent me a private note to call on him at the Legation. I did so, and stated what had occurred, and he was greatly pleased over what had been done. Senator Voorhees and I went to Baltimore again and again and again, for over four months, each time getting a show cause order, to which Marshal McClintock would reply with affidavits of the doctors.

" In June I called on President Cleveland, whom I had known in Buffalo.

" The Department of Justice ordered a second commission of United States surgeons to examine Stone. They did so, and reported that Stone could be moved with safety, from the fact that wherever the bullet was, it would be imbedded permanently now, and not apt to cause any trouble. This

113

examination was held on Friday, July 9th, and the report was made the next day. Tuesday, July 20th, was set as the date for the hearing before Commissioner Rogers. It was a memorable hearing in the history of extradition cases. For the prosecution appeared United States Senator Daniel W. Voorhees, Assistant Attorney-General of the United States Heber May, Paul Jones, a nephew of Voorhees, and United States District Attorney Thomas Hayes. For the defence appeared ex-Governor William Pinckney White, his son, and ex-Judge Garey, and W. M. Simpson. The hearing began on Tuesday, and continued every day until Saturday. The defence, as the Justice of the United States Supreme Court had foreseen, advanced the plea of insanity. To this the prosecution objected, and very rightly, stating that was for a jury, and not for a Commissioner, to determine ; and I believe that the Justices of the United States Supreme Court would have taken this view of it. The defence brought witnesses and doctors all the way from Texas to prove John Stone did remarkable and irrational things.

" They swore John Stone imagined at times that he was Napoleon, and that he rode with a cloak and sword on the prairies, that he reviewed imaginary armies, and that he delighted imaginary audiences. They swore Maude Hodge, the girl whom he had shot, and who had recovered, and her mother, Mrs. Maloma Hodge, who swore that on the day of the shooting John Stone's eyes were like those of a raving maniac. Hugh W. Matthews and Mrs. Matthews also were sworn. When it came to the arguments, a two-horse waggon would not carry off the law books used by counsel. I got a post-graduate course in extradition law that I never will forget. Commissioner Rogers decided John Stone was insane. I went to Washington.

" ' You'll appeal, won't you, Murray,' said Attorney-General Garland.

" ' Yes,' said I, ' but I must see the Attorney-General of Ontario first.'

"I returned to Toronto, and conferred with Premier Mowat. He thought we had done all in our power, and it would appear too vindictive, as if we were after blood, to push it further. If I had foreseen this I would not have conferred with him. I went back to Washington to settle up the matter. I called on Senator Voorhees, and we went to see Attorney-General Garland.

"'Murray's come here with a pocketful of Canada money,' said Voorhees to Garland jokingly. 'What shall we do; take it away from him?'

"'Oh, no,' said Attorney-General Garland. 'In respect to our friend, we'll bear the burden of these expenses, and his Government of course will appreciate the splendid work he has done.'

"Attorney-General Garland directed that all expenses, the Commissioner, Marshal, witnesses, doctors, and detectives, amounting to several thousand dollars, be paid by the United States. The three detectives were on duty watching Stone one hundred and thirty days. They received $5 each a day, or a total of $1,950. Chief Frey and his staff gave a banquet for me before I left. He and his men stood true through the entire case, and could not be swerved. They are of God's own people in the police business.

"John Stone was discharged in Baltimore. He went to Texas, as well as ever. Two years later eczema broke out, and shortly thereafter he died. The bullet was found imbedded in his brain. After hearing this, I investigated the matter of foreign substances in the brain. I found a case reported in New Hampshire where a man was blasting, the charge hung fire, he tampered with it, and the crowbar was blown up to the top of his head, so that two men had to pull it out, and yet he lived. A German case was reported where a man, desiring to commit suicide, drove two chisels into his head with a mallet. They caused him such pain that he yelled, and help came, and pulled them out, and he lived. Marvellous things happen to the brain, and the persons still live.

"The case of John Stone was remarkable, not alone for the bullet in the brain. John Stone was a remarkable man, with a brain full of stranger things than bullets, but we were entitled to a jury trial of his case, and in this I feel that my opinion would have been upheld by the Justices of the Supreme Court of the United States. I do not, of course, mean to say that I know whereof I speak. I heard Stone died in the midst of vain imaginings."

20

BATES OF ALLANBURG'S FUNERAL PYRE

DELUSIONS of grandeur adorned the closing years of the life of one of the picturesque country characters of Canada. He was Old Bates of Allanburg. He lived in a comfortable house with his wife, and the old couple were known widely in the county of Welland. Both were deaf. Old Bates had heart disease, and finally dropsy developed. To brighten his burdensome days the hand of affliction mercifully touched his mind, and thereafter the old man's troubles fell away.

"Dr. Blackstock, of Thorold, attended him for many months," says Murray. "The doctor's skill did much to make the old man comfortable. But he gave little heed to the actual affairs of life. He dwelt in an imaginary world peopled with strange beings. He saw a neighbouring farmer passing his house one day, and invited him to stay to tea. The farmer reluctantly accepted, lest he should offend the old man. Old Bates welcomed him with much ceremony, and bade him feel perfectly at home among the distinguished guests. All were personal friends of Old Bates.

"'Napoleon,' said Old Bates, speaking to the cupboard, 'this is a personal friend of mine'; and, continuing to the neighbour, he said: 'Shake hands with the Emperor. He's a little fellow, but he's ploughed a big furrow in his day.'

"After laughing and patting the imaginary Napoleon on the back, Old Bates led the neighbour aside, and pointing to a table said: 'That black moustached, handsome man is a villain and a scoundrel, and his weakness is slapping the faces of sunflowers. He is cruel to them.' Pointing to an ironing board he said: 'That tall man is a gentleman. He and I often chat together for hours in the night. He is in love with the moon.' Turning towards a chair, Old Bates

116

whispered: 'That fellow with the red scar on his face is an incendiary. He sets fires all over the world. He has stopped here on a visit to Napoleon, and is going away in a day or two. He's a very agreeable fellow in the winter, but in the summer he gets oppressive. That venerable, white-bearded fellow beyond him is a prophet and the son of a prophet. He knows all that is to happen, and forgets all that has happened. That pale-faced fellow in the corner is dying of fright; he has the fear fever. He is afraid of everything he sees, and of everything else because he cannot see it. He sleeps with a lighted candle at the head of the bed. If the night wind blows the candle out he will die. I sympathise with him. It is an awful thing to die in the dark. You cannot see where you are going. You may stumble into the wrong world in the hereafter. Napoleon says that he intends to make a lantern out of some stars when he goes.'

"Old Bates chatted confidentially with the neighbour and then with members of the invisible company. He bade them all look well at the neighbour, so they would know him if they ever met him again. Old Bates laughed with the imaginary incendiary, had a great joke with the tall gentleman, and engaged in a thoughtful, earnest discussion with the prophet. The people of his imagination lived and moved and had their being in his existence. Old Bates summoned them all to the table and told them to eat, drink, and be merry. He listened intently while the phantom Napoleon told of great war-fires he had kindled, and Old Bates applauded excitedly as he seemed to hear the fiery tale of flames roaring on all sides of an advancing army, devouring the land. He shook hands enthusiastically with Napoleon, and declared it was too bad he had not been born an Englishman.

"The neighbour humoured the old man, and after tea he went his way. Old Bates continued with the figures of his fancy, the old man ruling a motley company. He never was violent, but always was gentle and peaceable. They entertained him well, and at times they sang; for old Bates suddenly would burst into rollicking choruses and clasp hands with imaginary hands extended out of the world of unreality. The hobby of the old man was fire or light. He disliked the dark. He believed in brightness and brilliancy, and a sudden light or shining would delight him.

"On the morning of February 6th, 1886, neighbours who passed the house observed the windows were barricaded and all the doors were shut. There was no sign of Old Bates or his wife; but smoke from the chimney told that they were inside, and probably getting breakfast. The barricading was attributed to the whims of the old man, who may have withstood a heavy attack on his home from fancied foes in the night, or who might have rallied with Napoleon to fight again one of the mighty battles of the French Empire.

"That night the home of Old Bates burned. The neighbours saw the glare in the sky and hastened to the house, but were too late. It burned to the ground, leaving a waste of ashes and a cellar full of charred timbers. In a corner of the cellar sat Old Bates, dead, with a butcher's knife in his hand. Near by lay Mrs. Bates. She had been stabbed from head to foot, tattooed with knife-jabs. There was not a spot on her body as large as your hand that had not been stabbed or gashed with a knife.

"There was great excitement, of course, among the neighbours. They were divided as to how it had happened. Many believed a burglar or an incendiary had stolen in upon the old couple and robbed them, and murdered the old woman and thrown the old man into the cellar and then fired the house. In fact, this view spread until a fellow named Neil McKeague, who had been apprehended once in Chicago, was looked on as one who should be arrested. I satisfied myself absolutely that he was not near the Bates's place, and could not have reached there within some hours of the tragedy. It was difficult to persuade or convince many of the people of this. They had become aroused by the crime, and it had stirred them out of their calmer judgment, and they were ready to fasten suspicion or belief of guilt on any person available for a culprit. But the jury took our view of it, and McKeague was not held after the inquest.

"Then came an incident that served to justify fully our

course. A son of Mrs. Bates lived at Port Rowan. He said that on the night of the fire he was asleep in his bed in his home at Port Rowan, when, in a dream, he saw his father barricade the doors and windows, then stealthily approach the bed where his wife was sleeping and drag her out and make her kneel on the floor while he seized a knife and stabbed her from head to foot. Then, in the dream, the old man set fire to the house, his face brightening and his eyes gleaming as he saw the tiny flame creep over the floor and leap up and lick the bed and rush roaring through the house. In the dream, the son said, he saw his mother die; he heard her cry for help; he saw his father, knife in hand, sit calmly back and face the flames, as if he were gazing upon good friends. The son told the dream, in the morning, to his wife. While he was telling it, he said, the telegram came informing him of the fire, and of the finding of the bodies of Mrs. Bates and Old Bates. The son said the bodies were found precisely as he had seen them in the dream.

"This statement of the dream by the son was accepted as absolutely true by many of the people, and it put an end to any talk that an outsider had fired the house. Some of the country folk travelled miles to hear this story, and some looked upon the dream as a revelation to the son in order to prevent the arrest or trial of an innocent man.

"In this case I had some remarkable illustrations of the inaccuracy of the average man or woman's description of a person. Even when they know a person well, they fail to describe the person perfectly. In the Bates case, for instance, I had descriptions of Bates himself, in which he had a full beard, was smooth-shaven, had white hair, had black hair, was six feet tall, was four feet tall, walked with a crutch, had one leg, had one eye, and so on. Many folk are inclined to agree to your question, that is, to answer it in the affirmative. I remember that at some of the places I stopped I tried this, and the answers were 'yes' almost invariably.

"'He had a black moustache, had he?' I asked, about a supposed stranger seen a week before in that part of the country.

"'Yes,' was the reply.

"'And he had a big scar over his left eye?' I asked eagerly.

"'Yes,' was the reply.

"'And his hair was purplish over the forehead?' I went on excitedly.

"'Yes, kind of purplish,' was the reply.

"'On his left hand he had a sixth finger?' I exclaimed.

"'Yes, on his left hand,' was the reply.

"'It was all imaginary, of course. They meant well, and probably desired to be obliging, or did not wish to disappoint me. This incident supplies an exaggerated illustration of what I mean. If you should doubt the accuracy of this observation, select six acquaintances whom you know fairly well—not your most intimate friends, but six whom you see frequently. Jot down detailed descriptions of them in their absence; as to height, weight, colour of eyes and hair, and marks like visible scars or birth-marks. Then compare these descriptions with the originals. The test will be full of surprises. I have met people, on the other hand, who had a mere casual glance at a stranger, yet gave a description simply perfect in its accuracy and completeness of detail.

"The Bates case had no outsider in it. Old Bates did it alone. He may have been in the clutches of one of his invisible company at the time. The incendiary who set fires all over the world may have overpowered him. The villain who slapped the faces of sunflowers may have seized the butcher's knife and stabbed the old woman. The pale-faced fellow with the fever of fear upon him may have appealed to Old Bates not to let him die in the dark. The old man may have yielded to the plea and summoned Napoleon, and sat back calmly to face death, delighted that he also did not have to die in the dark."

21

A SPREADER OF ARSENIC

CATTLE poisoning in Canada is a crime certain to be punished severely. Some of the finest cattle in the world are bred in Ontario, and the province is watchful in its protection of them. Near Cortland village, in the county of Norfolk, in 1886, Dr. McKay, a breeder and raiser of fancy stock, had a choice herd on a large tract of land. There were beauties in the herd, and the doctor justly was proud of them.

" In the spring of that year a number of the doctor's fine cattle died suddenly," says Murray. " They had not been sick or off their feed, and their unexpected death immediately aroused the doctor's suspicions. A week later, more of the cattle died in the same manner. They dropped as if struck by invisible lightning. The doctor notified the department. I suspected poisoning, and went to investigate. I obtained the viscera of some of the cattle, and had an analysis made, and it revealed the presence of arsenic in large quantities. That proved positively the poisoning theory. The probable way for giving arsenic would be with the salt. Cattle love salt, and when it is sprinkled on the ground they will lick the earth to get it. The traces of salt were not easily found when I arrived, but I discovered one spot that still showed traces of it, and I carefully dug it up, and had the top of the earth analysed, and faint traces of arsenic were found. In some of the spots where the cattle had fallen dead the grass had been licked to the ground.

" All that summer the cattle kept dying. They would go out in the morning healthy and strong, and suddenly drop dead in the field or by the roadside. I talked with Dr. McKay, and asked him if he ever had any quarrel or trouble

121

with a neighbour. He recalled one man, Robert Morrow, who lived near, and who formerly had taken contracts from the doctor for draining or otherwise improving the doctor's land. On one occasion, a year or more before, Morrow became dissatisfied over a contract, and sued the doctor. Dr. McKay said he had offered to leave the matter to arbitration or to one or three of the neighbours, but Morrow wanted law, and told the doctor that if he did not pay him what he asked he would get even with him. Months passed, and suddenly the doctor's cattle began to die.

"I met Morrow casually, and I did not like his looks. I placed two men to watch Morrow all that summer. The months went by, and they could not catch him. The cattle kept dying, and finally in December of that year I went to Cortland, and took up the matter of Morrow's actions. There was no spot near his house convenient for hiding except a tree. So I sent a man, who slipped up in the twilight, and climbed the tree, and waited. For three nights I did this unknown to any one, and Morrow never so much as stuck his head out of the door. On the fourth night, after one o'clock in the morning, my watcher heard the door open softly, and a figure slipped out and started along in the shadow of the fence. My watcher waited until he was well started, and then slid down out of the tree. As he began to slide his coat caught and held him. It was a lucky catch, for, as he drew himself up, he saw the figure stealthily sneaking round the house. It was Morrow, and he was investigating his own premises to make sure he was not being watched. The watcher sat silent on his perch in the tree and saw him enter the house, then reappear, carrying a small bag. He glided away in the darkness, and my man followed. The pursuer fancied he heard him once, but was careful not to crowd upon him. The result was, he lost him.

"Along a fence near McKay's he disappeared, and the watcher crawled to and fro, looking for him in vain. At length he gave him up, and crept out into McKay's field, and there came upon newly laid salt. In fact, he had his hands in it before he discovered it. He carefully brushed up enough to fill a cup. This he put in a bag, and tucked away in his pocket. Then he went to McKay's, and told them not to turn out any cattle in that particular field. It was daylight when he reported to me. I started at once to Morrow's.

"Morrow was standing outside when I approached the house.

"'Good morning,' said I.

"'Morning to you,' said he. 'Nice day.'

"'Fine,' said I. 'By the way, where did this salt in McKay's field come from?' and I produced the bag.

"Morrow gasped, then paled—I almost pitied him. He stared, and shook like a man with the ague. I waited. He twitched, and shivered, and gasped.

"'Are you ill?' I asked him.

"'I don't feel well this morning,' said he. 'Bilious; bad stomach; indigestion.'

"'Ah!' said I. 'Salt's just the thing. Nothing like salt to fix the stomach. Have some?' and I held up the bag.

"Morrow shrank as if I had offered to shoot him through the heart. He clapped one hand to his mouth, and suddenly began to hiccup. He actually grew sick, gulping like a landlubber in a heavy sea. I pocketed the salt and went over to him.

"'Some of this salt was on the food you ate for breakfast,' I said, for he was so flustered he did not know what was coming next. 'You must have eaten it.'

"He writhed and moaned. He verily seemed to fear he had been poisoned. While he retched and groaned I searched his house and found arsenic. I arrested him, and told him to stop belching, as he was not going to die. He was as relieved as a man reprieved on the gallows. The black cap of death seemed lifted from his head when he learned he had not eaten of the salt he had poisoned.

"I took Morrow to Simcoe gaol, and on December 22nd he was committed for trial. He was tried before Judge Matthew Cruiks Cameron at the Spring Assizes in 1887, and was sent to Kingston Penitentiary for seven years. I not only had the evidence of the arsenic in his house, but I learned also where he bought the arsenic. Dr. McKay lost over fifty head of cattle, but all of them combined did not suffer agonies equal to those endured by Morrow on the morning he retched and moaned in the belief that he had eaten of his own poisoned mess. It was drastic, but deserved. Morrow had an imaginary taste of his own mixing. It stirred him to the innermost parts of his being. He almost gave up the ghost."

22

FOR A MESS OF POTTAGE

BEN HAGAMAN was his mother's pet. She coddled him as a child, and pampered him as a youth. His father was a rich merchant of Ridgetown, Ontario, and his brother-in-law was a prosperous, successful business man. His uncle was Benjamin Hagaman, the Chicago millionaire, who was a bachelor, and after whom young Ben had been named.

"Young Ben stood to inherit old Ben's fortune," says Murray. "He was a sunny-tempered, merry, good-looking, likeable young fellow, and his shrewd, rich old uncle was very fond of him. All Ben needed to do was to learn the ways of business under his uncle's supervision, and in due time he would inherit millions. Young Ben knew this. His uncle took him when he was of age and taught him something of business, and in the course of giving him practical experience old Ben sent young Ben out to Fargo, North Dakota, and made him paying teller in his bank there. Young Ben seemed to do well, but one day he unexpectedly returned to Canada and settled down again at the old home. No word came from old Ben, and no explanation was given by young Ben. In due time young Ben had married, and had two children.

"Sir William P. Howland, of Toronto, ex-Lieutenant-Governor of the Province, met young Ben. Sir William was the head of Howland, Jones & Co., and had large flour mills at Thorold. He needed a book-keeper there, and when young Ben, son of the rich Ridgetown merchant and nephew of the Chicago multi-millionaire, applied to him, he employed Ben in the capacity not only of book-keeper, but confidential clerk at the Thorold mills. Sir William instructed young Ben to keep an eye on Sir William's partner, who was as honest a man as the sun ever shone upon. Young Ben nodded wisely, aware instantly that

Sir William might distrust his partner despite their close relations.

"Young Ben quickly familiarised himself with his duties. He learned that grain was bought by the carload, and was paid for by cheques drawn by the book-keeper and signed by Mr. Jones, Sir William's partner. Young Ben was deft with a pen. After the arrival of a consignment of grain valued at $470, young Ben wrote out a cheque with a little interval after the 'four' in the 'four hundred and seventy.' He took the cheque to Mr. Jones, who signed it as usual. Young Ben then took the signed cheque and added 'teen' to the 'four,' making it read 'fourteen hundred and seventy,' and put a '1' after the '$' before the '470,' making it $1,470, and thereby raising the cheque $1,000. He arranged the indorsement also, and sent it through the bank. Between September and December, 1886, young Ben did this sixteen times, getting $1,000 each time, or $16,000, apart from the amount actually due for grain. On December 20th he went away, saying he would be back on the 22nd. He did not return, and the firm's balance at the bank showed $16,000 missing. Before disappearing Ben made a farewell visit to Toronto, where he bought some elegant jewellery from W. P. Ellis, including some costly diamonds. Part of the jewellery he succeeded in obtaining on credit.

"Sir William was dumfounded. He could not bring himself to believe that young Ben had robbed him. Yet there were the cheques, each for $1,000 more than the proper amount. Mr. Jones was sure they had been raised after he had signed them. Finally the matter came to my attention, and on January 24th, 1887, I took it up. I first learned that old Ben, the Chicago millionaire, had washed his hands of his precious namesake after young Ben had made away with some $4,000 or $5,000 not belonging to him in the Fargo bank. Old Ben had said that ended it between him and his nephew, and he had packed young Ben back home. If young Ben had straightened out and worked steadily, old Ben would have taken him again, for the uncle was fond of the nephew, and was greatly pleased when young Ben went to work for Sir William P. Howland.

" I traced young Ben to Michigan, then to Chicago, and then to Denver. He had money, and spent it freely. He started out as B. Hatfield, then he became W. T. Schufeldt then he called himself Frank Bruce, and next he was masquerading as J. Peter Sonntag. I telegraphed his description all over the country, and heard from him under these names as having been in these places. His description was such that it was easy to identify him ; and so long as he had money he would be in public places, for he was a lavish spender, a high liver, and a gay sport. The love of high living was one of the roots of his evil. I conferred with the Pinkerton people, who also were looking for young Ben, and finally I prepared extradition papers and started for the States, and Ben was arrested in San Francisco as he was taking steamer to leave the country. Instead of J. Peter Sonntag, or any of his other aliases, Ben at this time gave the name of plain P. Sontag.

" Benny Peter Sontag Hagaman had been living a merry life in San Francisco. He was a thoroughbred in the Pacific Coast city. He frequented Patsy Hogan's, and was in with the swiftest boys in the town. He had hired a box in a safety vault in a trust company, and had deposited in it thousands of dollars in cash, and a lot of diamonds and jewellery. I arrived in San Francisco on February 1st. Sir William P. Howland had telegraphed to some friend of his to engage counsel. His friend had engaged Davis Louderback, and he did not prove very satisfactory. I appeared on February 2nd before United States Commissioner Sawyer. Ben was arraigned, and remanded for eight days. He prepared to fight extradition, and W. W. Bishop defended him. Bishop, Ben's lawyer, and Louderback, my lawyer, hired by Sir William's friend, visited the prisoner several times in gaol. Everything uttered before the Commissioner was ordered to be taken down, until there were volumes of evidence. Ben was remanded for extradition, and I was informed the papers had gone to Washington for the warrant of surrender. I waited and heard nothing, and promptly telegraphed to the British Legation at Washington that the forms of the treaty had been complied with and copies of the proceedings had been sent to the State Department, and I asked that the warrant of surrender be sent to me as soon as possible. Sir Sackville West replied that inquiry at the State Department showed no papers had arrived there in the case, and the Department knew nothing of it. I called on Louderback, and got very little satisfaction out of him.

"I then called on Commissioner Sawyer. He was a nephew of Judge Sawyer. He said the papers had not been sent to Washington, and had to be paid for before they would be transmitted. He said the charge was $150. I told him I would pay if he would give me an itemised bill. He refused, but finally gave me a receipt for $150. The papers were so bulky that the postage on them was $11. The postmaster was quite unlike some of the other people I met in San Francisco, and he treated me most courteously, and franked the papers for me, which the Commissioner had refused to do.

"While I was waiting for the warrant of surrender to arrive from Washington, I began to puzzle over what further steps might be taken to get young Ben out. I knew that the money he had would be of great value to him in this emergency, and I finally concluded that it was quite possible for young Ben to be brought in on a writ of *habeas corpus* and discharged without my knowledge, in the event of a failure of counsel to notify me. So I went over the heads of all the lawyers and lesser officials, and called on Judges Sawyer and Hofman and stated the whole case to them, explaining how I considered I was handicapped. They told me there would be no discharge of young Ben on a writ of *habeas corpus*, and I breathed easier. The warrant of surrender had arrived, and on March 26th I left San Francisco with young Ben. Before leaving I began a civil suit to return the money and diamonds which the police meanwhile had taken into their keeping. I had Sir William P. Howland employ other counsel, and they recovered over $5,000.

"When young Ben arrived home he was released on $8,000 bail, pending his trial. He came to Toronto while he was out on bail, and called on me for advice. He asked me what he had better do under the circumstances. He wanted my honest opinion, so I gave him a gentle hint.

"'Ben,' said I, 'you have spent $11,000 of another man's money, and you have put him to great trouble. Your father is rich, your brother-in-law is rich, your uncle is a millionaire. The other man wants his money. If you want to go to the penitentiary, don't pay him; but if you want to keep out of the penitentiary——'

"'What! Pay old Howland $11,000?' said young Ben, and he laughed uproariously. 'Not on your life. I'll beat Sir Bill, and I'll not go to the penitentiary either.'

"Foolish young man! I told him so at the time. But he was at the age when all who are younger have it to learn, and all who are older have forgotten what they once knew. He went his way, pig-headed, obstinate, self-willed, and a fool—a pleasant, bright, intelligent, likeable fool. His trial came on at the Spring Assizes in 1888. Colin McDougal, an able lawyer, defended him; but he was prosecuted by one of the most brilliant criminal lawyers Canada has produced, the late B. B. Osler. Young Ben was convicted, and was sent to the Kingston penitentiary for seven years.

"I saw him once or twice in the penitentiary. One of the old-time Sunday School texts was 'The way of the transgressor is hard.' Young Ben had it on the wall of his cell. It certainly was true of him. He came of a refined, rich family, in which he was the mother's darling and a spoiled child. He was to inherit millions, and he sold his birthright for a mess of pottage. He stole $4,000 and then $16,000, and thereby sold more than $1,000,000 for $20,000, of which he had to repay over $5,000. So he forfeited a fortune for $15,000. There was no need for him to steal. He had all of life's good things essential to the joy of living—a happy home, a fine family, a lucrative position, and good health. After he fled his two little children died, and after he went to the penitentiary his wife got a divorce, and remarried; and when he came out into the world and his uncle died, leaving no will, instead of finding himself a millionaire he left Canada a branded man. It was an awful lesson. It began simply in a love for gay company, and it ended in solitude in a stone-walled cell."

23

"SHET-BLACK HERRES OF THE DING-DONG MUSTACHEES"

A SING-SONG voiced, jet-black haired, sanctimonious scalawag named J. K. Herres lived near Aylmer in the county of Waterloo. His father kept a country store, and was reputed to be fairly well off. When young Herres was not teaching a little school or singing German songs he was gallivanting about the country. He had a profuse rush of hair to the upper lip, and he developed a particular fondness for twirling the drooping ends of his mustaches. He seemed so insipid that one never would have imagined him to be the child of destiny in a stirring event where a whole town turned out to rescue him, while his captor, with drawn guns, backed against a wall with Herres at his feet, and prepared to sell his life as dearly as possible.

"Herres frequently went to Galt in his Lochinvarring tours," says Murray. "In the summer of 1887 he walked into the office of John Cavers, manager of the branch of the Imperial Bank at Galt, and presented two notes to be discounted. One was signed by Peter Leweller, a neighbour of the Herres family, and the other by Herres's father. They totalled $900, and Mr. Cavers discounted them. Herres vanished with the money. Old man Herres and Peter Leweller pronounced their signatures forgeries. The case came to me, and on September 22nd I went to Galt, saw Manager Cavers, and thence went to Berlin, the county seat of Waterloo. There I prepared extradition papers, and obtained from Chief Constable John Klippert, of Waterloo, a description of Herres. Klippert was one of the best constables in Canada, a shrewd old German.

"'Shon,' he said to me, 'you vill know him two ways, one by his shet-black hair and one by his ding-dong mustachees. He has some of the lofliest mustachees you efer see. They flow down like Niagara Falls, only they, too, are shet-black.'

" 'But suppose he has shaved them off?' I said.

" 'You vill know t'em by the place where they once used to be,' said Klippert. 'And remember—shet-black!'

" I telegraphed all over the country for a trace of Herres, and found none. I learned that he had a cousin who was a lawyer at White Cloud, in Minnesota, and Shet-Black Herres, as I called him ever after hearing Klippert's description, had been in correspondence with this cousin, whose address was found in an old coat belonging to Herres. I decided to visit White Cloud. On September 28th I started for St. Paul. On arrival there I called at Police Headquarters and on United States Commissioner Spencer, and prepared the necessary warrant for Herres, if I should find him. I also called on my friend United States Marshal Campbell, who gave me a letter to Congressman C. F. McDonald, of White Cloud, a prominent man in that part of the country. I went to White Cloud and looked up the cousin of Herres. I learned from neighbours that the cousin had a visitor sometime before, a dapper fellow with a remarkably fine mustache. He had tarried only a few days, and then had driven away. He had not shaved it off was my glad thought. I called on Congressman McDonald, and he gave me letters to prominent people within a radius of a couple of hundred miles. Part of the country round about was thinly settled at that time. I set out to find the man with the fine mustache.

" It was like looking for a needle in a haystack. I travelled all around the country. I saw more smooth-shaven men and more men with beards than I imagined were in that part of the country, but not one man with 'ding-dong mustachees' did I see. I returned to White Cloud without clue or trace of my man. I learned then of a settlement of Germans at Little Falls, and I remembered what I had heard of Herres's fondness for German songs ; and one man in White Cloud thought Herres's cousin had a relative in this settlement. Little Falls was several hundred miles from St. Paul, and I arrived there on October 4th. It was a little place of about one thousand people, and I think I saw everybody in the town. I found no trace of Herres and was about to give up the chase there, when the school-teaching side of Herres came again to my mind. The idea struck me to try the schools. I did so—no Herres. But there were country schools. I called on a storekeeper who was one of the school trustees. Yes, some teachers had been employed for country schools. The clerk of the school board lived near by, he said, and I should see him. To the clerk I went. He immediately wanted to know the names of the teachers I sought. I said I did not recall the names. He said two teachers had been appointed to little rural schools about forty miles out in the country. Both teachers were strangers to him. He gave me their names. Neither was named Herres.

" 'One was smooth-shaven, one I did not see,' he said.

" I decided to look at the two teachers. There was a big fellow named Richardson in the town, a sort of marshal or town policeman or constable. He said he knew the country all around there, as he had been born there. I hired a splendid team from a liveryman, a pair of as good horses as a man could wish to drive, with a light cracky waggon. The liveryman lent me his gun and shooting jacket, cartridge belt and two valuable dogs. I told Richardson we were going shooting. Prairie chickens were thicker than flies. We started on Wednesday, October 5th. We drove about twenty miles to the cross-roads of nowhere. It was dark when we trotted out of Little Falls, and we breakfasted at a cross-roads store on the way. I told Richardson, after we were well on the road, the real purpose of my trip. It seemed to make him as solemn as an owl. He was a jolly hunter, but a solemn policeman. Many men are that way. Their business is something awesome or deadly serious, but apart from it they are good fellows.

" At length we came to the first school. The teacher was a little fellow, a Frenchman, and he could not speak German. He was not Herres, and we drove on to the next district school. The little Frenchman told me of the teacher.

132

"'He has ze long moostache,' he said. 'Very fine, oh very fine. Ze long moostache, and I haf ze no moostache at all,' and he clasped his hands and sighed.

"I was sure the other teacher was Herres. When we came in sight of the school I unhitched the horses and tied them, and cut across toward the school-house.

"'If this is the fellow, I will nod to you and you arrest him,' I said to Richardson.

"'I have no authority,' he said, 'and I will not arrest a man without authority,' and I saw he meant it.

"'Richardson,' I said solemnly, 'I am a United States Marshal. I hereby declare you my deputy. You must obey the law and serve.'

"'But I must be sworn in,' said Richardson.

"I pulled out a bundle of papers, ran over them, selected one and told him to kneel down. He knelt amid the briers. I mumbled the form of an oath.

"'I do,' he answered solemnly, to my question of, 'Do you so swear?'

"Then we went on to the school-house and walked in. There stood the teacher, dapper and with a 'ding-dong mustachees,' but instead of being 'shet-black' his hair and mustache were brown. He was a bleached Herres. 'It looks like him,' said I to myself, 'and yet, is it he?' Just then he twirled his mustache. That settled it. There were about thirty children, mostly girls, in the room. They eyed us curiously.

"'Teacher, how long have you been here?' said I.

"'For some time—since school opened,' said he, and his voice had a little sing-song.

"'What is your name?'

"'John Walker,' he replied.

"'When did you leave Canada?' I asked.

"'I have never been in Canada in my life,' he said.

"I looked at his school-books. All were marked John Walker.

"'Are you German?' I asked.

"'Yes,' said he.

"'John Walker is not a German name,' I said.

133

" He smiled.

" ' You are from Canada!' I said abruptly.

" ' I am not!' he exclaimed, and turning to the astonished children, he told them to go out and get their fathers. 'Bring them quickly,' he said, speaking rapidly in German to the children. 'Tell them to bring their guns. There are robbers here.'

" I understood him clearly, and I told Richardson to keep the children in. Deputy Marshal Richardson obeyed by standing against the door. The children began to cry, then to scream.

" ' That's right!' said the teacher to the children. 'Shout for help! Shout as loud as you can!'

" The whole school began to yell. They ran round the room shrieking and screaming.

" ' Keep your seats and scream,' said the teacher.

" They promptly sat down and howled at the top of their voices for help.

" ' Come with me,' said I to the teacher.

" ' I will not,' said he, and he whipped off his coat.

" I leaped for him, and down we went, upsetting the table and rolling over the floor. He was an active fellow, and I had to drag him out of the school-house.

" ' Keep the children in,' said I to Richardson, ' until I fire a shot, then run as fast as you can to the waggon.'

" The teacher quieted down after I got him outside, but I had to drag him across to the waggon. I tied him to a wheel, handcuffed, while I hitched up the horses. Then I lifted him into the waggon and fired the gun. The gun scared him, and he sat quiet. I could see Richardson come running, and I could see the screaming children stream out of the school-house and rush, yelling for help, in all directions. Richardson fell on the way and got tangled in some briers, and after considerable delay he reached the waggon and clambered in.

" ' Drive to the nearest railroad station," I said, and Richardson whipped up the horses and away we went on the road to Royalton, over thirty miles away.

" We could hear the cries of the children dying away as

134

we went.

" 'You'll suffer for this, sir,' said the school-teacher to me. 'You will pay for dragging an honest man about like this.'

" I looked him all over, and to tell the truth I felt shaky myself. We got into Royalton late in the afternoon. It was a German settlement of perhaps fifteen hundred population. We drove to the railroad station. The telegraph operator was a German. When the school-teacher spied the telegraph operator he began to yell in German to send a message saying he was kidnapped by robbers. The operator wanted to help him. The school-teacher shouted in German.

" 'Save me! Save me! I am being kidnapped! Help! Help!' he shouted, as loud as he could yell.

" A crowd gathered. It grew rapidly. All the while the school-teacher kept yelling with all the power of voice and lungs. The crowd began to murmur. I moved back against the side of the station, keeping the school-teacher beside me.

" 'Richardson, keep the crowd back,' I said, but Richardson decided he wanted nothing more to do with the affair.

" ' I resign as deputy marshal,' he said.

" The crowd drew in closer. I could see men galloping into town, and I knew they were farmers who had been aroused by their children's tale of the struggle in the school-house. They dismounted and told the story given by the children. The crowd surged in. I had the shot gun and a revolver, with another revolver in my pocket. I discarded the shot gun and drew a second revolver. All the while the school-teacher kept haranguing the crowd, inciting them to hang me and praying to them to rescue him. The mob actually surrounded the station.

" 'Give up that man,' demanded one of their number, a sturdy fellow not twenty feet from me.

" 'The first man of you who touches him or me dies in his tracks,' I said, while the school-teacher begged them to rescue him from my clutches.

" 'Do not let him take an innocent man to be murdered,' shrieked the school-teacher.

" The crowd surged in. I gripped both revolvers, thinking, 'Here she comes; steady, old man, steady,' and I decided that the bleating school-teacher would be one of us on the other side when they picked up the bodies.

"'Stand back! Stand back!' I shouted, at bay, one man standing off a whole town.

"I flourished the guns, then levelled them, and just as I expected to have the crash come, a big fellow burst through the crowd.

"'What's up?' he said, as his eyes took in the braying school-teacher, handcuffed at my feet, the surging crowd and myself, up against the station wall, a revolver in each hand.

"The big fellow's hands flew to his hip pockets. Out flipped two guns as he sprang over beside me and backed up against the wall.

"'A thousand to one,' he chuckled. 'God, but you're a game man.' He looked out of two fearless blue eyes at the crowd. 'Come on, you villains!' he shouted. 'Come on! Who'll be the first to die?'

"It was superb. The man was a whirlwind in his way.

"'I'm Quinn, sheriff of the next county,' he said to me rapidly. 'What's it all about?'

"'I am an officer from St. Paul, and these people are after my prisoner,' I said.

"'So ho!' said Quinn. 'Well, they don't get him.'

"He eyed the crowd.

"'Get back! Back up!' he shouted. 'Back up or I'll back you up! One—two——' he counted.

"The crowd began to give, and the space in front of us grew as Quinn counted one and two. He laughed and I laughed. I turned to the telegraph operator and told him to take a dispatch as I dictated it and send it at once. As we stood, revolvers in hand, backed up against the station beside the telegraph office, I sent a telegram to Marshal Campbell saying we would arrive in St. Paul by the next train.

"'It gets in at one o'clock in the morning,' said Quinn, and I put the hour in the dispatch.

"Richardson came up then, and I gave him the shot gun and money to pay the liveryman, and he drove away; and later I wrote to the liveryman, who replied that all was satisfactory. Quinn stood by until the train arrived, and he boarded it with me and rode to the third station beyond, where he left me, with a hearty handshake and a laugh when I thanked him. The school-teacher had subsided, except to remind me occasionally that I would suffer for treating an innocent man in this way. He may have realised how close to death he was on that station platform. Marshal Campbell met us at the train at one o'clock in the morning in St. Paul.

" 'This is Herres,' I said to Campbell.

" Up spoke the school-teacher, as if he were about to shout again for a crowd of rescuers.

" ' My name is not Herres; my name is John Walker,' he said. ' Some one will pay for this.'

" It shook Campbell. We stepped aside.

" ' Are you certain he is Herres ?' asked Campbell.

" ' I am not certain, but I'm fairly sure,' said I. ' His hair is lighter. But I'll be responsible.'

" Campbell locked up the school-teacher. John Walker immediately sent for Colonel Kerr of St. Paul, to defend him. He also engaged a fighting lawyer named Ryan. They wanted to get a change of venue. I had United States District-Attorney George N. Baxter as my counsel. In making the affidavit on the application for a change of venue they swore the school-teacher to it. He signed it. Campbell and I eagerly looked at it. The signature was J. K. Herres ! The marshal and I silently shook hands and went out and had a drink. It took a great load off me. The Court denied the change of venue sought on the unjust allegation that Commissioner Spencer was a friend of Canada officers. Then began the battle for extradition.

" It was fought to a finish. Herres's cousin in White Cloud joined Colonel Kerr and Mr. Ryan. Herres was committed for extradition. His counsel applied for a writ of *habeas corpus* before Judge Nelson. It seemed that when Judge Nelson's father was Judge of the Supreme Court a man named Kane had killed some one in Ireland and escaped to Minnesota. The British Government sought to extradite him, and the case was carried to the Supreme Court, which held that it was necessary to have the President issue an

137

executive mandate to give the Commissioner power to try the case. The counsel for Herres claimed the proceeding in the Herres case was irregular, and Judge Nelson discharged Herres. We appealed from the decision of Judge Nelson and carried it to the Circuit Court before Judge Brewer, now Justice Brewer of the Supreme Court of the United States. Judge Brewer wrote a long opinion reversing Judge Nelson's judgment and ordering the prisoner back into my custody. This case is an authority in extradition cases, and is reported in Federal Reports of the United States, No. 33, page 265. We fought the matter in the courts through November and December 1887, and finally the warrant of surrender arrived ; and on January 17th, 1888, I left St. Paul with Shet-black Herres, and handed him over in Berlin on Thursday, January 19th. He pleaded not guilty to forgery at the Spring Assizes, but was convicted and sentenced on March 20th to seven years in Kingston, where his 'ding-dong mustachee' vanished before the razor of the prison barber.

" He had dyed his 'shet-black' hair with butternut dye. It made his hair a nasty yellow and seemed to me to symbolise the make-up of Herres. The two meanest prisoners I ever had were this Shet-black Herres and a fellow named Drinkwater. Herres was a mean cuss. He was not a finish fighter like some desperate, courageous men, out in the open. He was a skulker, and a mean one. While in gaol at St. Paul he acted so badly with the officials that some fellow, a little insane, was put in the cell with Shet-black Herres and committed all kinds of nuisances over him. Shet-black began an action against the sheriff in St. Paul, but it failed. Shet-black was serving seven years in Kingston instead of suing the good sheriff of St. Paul. But greatest of all his griefs was the loss of his 'ding-dong mustachee !'"

24

OLD JOHN KLIPPERT OF WATERLOO

JOHN KLIPPERT was the Pooh Bah of the county of Waterloo. He filled many offices, and filled them ably too. He was chief constable and crier of the court and bailiff and issuer of marriage licences and deputy sheriff, and several other officials, all in one. He was a keen, shrewd fellow, abrupt in his manner and picturesque in his speech. He had sandy hair and a sandy mustache, and he used to toddle along with his head well forward, conversing amiably with himself. The county of Waterloo was known to him from end to end, every nook and corner. It is a rich county, and among its settlers was a colony of sturdy German loyalists who moved from Pennsylvania to Ontario in the early days of the history of the United States. Klippert was of German ancestry, and he reminded his hearers constantly of the fact by his entertaining English.

" The farms of the county of Waterloo were well stocked," says Murray, " and in 1888 horses began to disappear. The stealing increased, until Mr. Snyder, the member of Parliament from Waterloo, spoke to me about the matter. Klippert also had written to me about it and described some of the horses. I knew where old Chisholm was, and settled first of all that he could not have been mixed up in it. Klippert worried me as time passed, and he pestered me with letters. At length I telegraphed him to get a warrant and come to Toronto. Old John arrived on the early train next day. It was Fair-time in Toronto. Detective Burrows had seen James Little, a notorious horse thief and head of a bad family, at the fair grounds the day before. Little had a son Tom, who was a highwayman.

" I sent Old John out to the fair grounds. Little had been trying to sell a couple of horses. Burrows spied him and pointed him out to old John. Klippert drew back about one hundred feet and carefully took out his handcuffs and carried them under his coat tails.

"Then he advanced stealthily, as if about to sprinkle salt on a bird's tail. Old Little was gazing at the crowd, when suddenly a hand was thrust into his face and a hoarse voice said :

"'Surrender!'

"Old John compelled old Little to hold out his wrists and be handcuffed. Then he led him over in triumph, and I met them.

"'I got him!' he exclaimed.

"Even old Little laughed.

"'What is the case against me?' he asked.

"That puzzled old John. He called me aside, keeping a watchful eye on old Little.

"'What case do I haf on him, Shon?' he asked.

"'You'll have to work it up,' I said, to have some fun. 'I'm sure he's your man, but you'll have to prove it.'

"I intended to send the witnesses to Berlin, the county seat of Waterloo, the next day. So I told Klippert to take old Little to Berlin and work out the case. The old constable was perplexed, but he took it seriously and bade me good-bye.

"'Come on,' he said to Little.

"What happened then I learned afterwards from both Klippert and Little. On the train old John began to talk of Little's hard luck.

"'Too bad, too bad,' said old John. 'I'm sorry to haf to take you back. T'at Vaterloo is a bad county for horse stealers. T'e shuries t'ey is yust death on horse thieves. T'ey socks it to a man, und t'ey always asks t'e shudge to sock it to him. T'at is part of t'e verdict, a plea from t'e shury to t'e shudge to sock it to t'e stealers and t'e thievers.'

"Old Little listened while honest old John told him of how the farmers hated a horse thief, and how they tried to get them sent down for twenty years, and how they were stirred up by recent thefts so that they were ready, almost, to take the thief out of gaol and string him up to the limb of a tree. The more old John, in his simple, broken way, talked of the tense state of affairs in the county, the more impressed was old Little over the dangers of his predicament.

" ' Ven ve get to Berlin I yust will see you safe in gaol, and tell no one but t'e shudge who you are und vat I got you for,' said old John.

" Little asked old John if it was necessary to tell the judge about his record. Klippert said it depended. If Little desired to take a jury trial, all the facts of his career would have to come out. If Little wished to make no trouble and take a speedy trial before the judge, without a jury, his past would not necessarily have to come out.

" ' Of course,' said old John, 't'e case I haf on you is so plain t'at t'ere vill be no use to fight it. I yust show t'e shudge t'e evidence, und he say "guilty." '

" Old Little told John he would take a speedy trial if old John would not rake up his record, and if he would put in a good word with the judge to get him off.

" ' Yah, yah,' said John. ' I will fix t'e shudge. You vas a vise man.'

" So old John took old Little before County Judge Da Costa and charged him with horse stealing.

" ' I plead guilty,' said old Little.

" The judge withdrew to a side room. Old John went in to see him a moment, and then returned to old Little.

" ' T'e shudge he vant to know if you vas honest,' said old John. ' I say yah, you vas. T'e shudge he ask me vere you sold t'e horse. Vat shall I tell him? Shall I tell him t'e right place or some wrong place?'

" ' Tell him the right place,' said old Little. ' You know— Burns's coal yard in Toronto.'

" Old John went back, and later old Little was brought up for sentence. Klippert meanwhile had telegraphed to Toronto and located the horse, and its owner identified it. Then old John, when Little was to be sentenced, said to the judge :

" ' Shudge, t'is man iss an old villain. His whole family

141

t'ey is stealers und thieves. He ought to go to prison for life.'

"Old John painted old Little so black that the notorious old horse thief did not even recognise his own record.

"The judge sent Little to Kingston for seven years. Klippert was delighted.

"' I worked out my case ; eh, Shon ? ' he said to me, and chuckled.

"Old Little was sore as a bear with the toothache. He blamed himself for being caught by old John's honest, blunt manner.

"' There's no fool like an old fool,' said Little, ' and I am the old one in this case.'

"From Klippert's view-point it was all right. He worked up his case after he got his man. As to the change of front towards old Little, every man must be his own arbiter in such matters. The man who would achieve the greatest success in the detective business must keep his word absolutely when he gives it. Oftentimes confidence of others in his word will bring success where otherwise there would be failure. The detective who breaks his word is marked among crooks just as among other men—in fact, he is marked more clearly and more disastrously. If he does not wish to keep his word, he should not give it.

"John Klippert, however, viewed the case from his stand-point, and his course appeared all right. He never saw Little before and he never expected to see him again ; and his business was to protect his county and show no favour to those who showed no favour to it. He used to chuckle over the case, and often spoke of it. Klippert was a faithful, efficient man. Old Little finally forgave him, and wrote him a letter, saying :

"' If I had a horse I would drive to Berlin and see you.'

"Old John sent word to him that if he ever set foot in the county of Waterloo the farmers would string him up by his heels and pitchfork him into eternity upside down. Old Little must have believed him, for he never poked his nose into Waterloo thereafter.

"Klippert was with me on an occasion when I bade as

142

dapper a little crook, as ever did wrong, to keep out of Canada. The affair began in the old days back in Erie. A suave, polished little fellow stepped off a train one day in Erie and registered at the Reed House as J. O. Flanders. He was as pleasant as could be, and made friends quickly. I met him and played billiards with him, and we became well acquainted. He said he was connected with the Claflins in New York, and he soon knew the leading merchants of Erie. He made friends particularly with Church, the merchant, producing a forged letter of introduction, and one day he went to Currie's bank, with Church to identify him, and deposited a draft for $30,000. The next day he went to the bank alone and drew $25,000, and skipped with the money. The draft turned out to be worthless. We set out to find him. Not a trace of him could we get. If he had kept out of women troubles, we never would have landed him. But he stole another crook's woman, and that made the other crook angry ; and we were tipped that J. O. Flanders was living in grand style at the Spencer House at Indianapolis, in Indiana. Crowley and I went out there to take Flanders back to Erie.

"Never had I seen such a complete change of appearance as there was in J. O. Flanders. His own mother would not have known him for the man who was in Erie. Hair, complexion, walk, manner, all were changed. He had plenty of money, and over $22,000 was found on him. He was taken before Judge Morris, who, to our great surprise, released him. We appealed, but Flanders had taken his $22,000 and was gone, and we returned to Erie. Nine months later he was caught in Fort Wayne. His $22,000 had vanished and he had $200 when arrested. Crowley and I went after him a second time and he was safe in gaol. The night before I was to take him away he thumped a gaoler on the head, stunning him, and escaped. I thought at the time the gaoler was in on the game. Then I returned to Erie in disgust, and said I was through monkeying with Flanders.

"Several years later, when I was with the Canada Southern Railroad, F. N. Finney and I walked into Strong's Hotel at London, Ontario, and who should be back of the desk as clerk but my old friend J. O. Flanders.

" ' Great God ! ' he whispered to me. ' Are you after me again ? '

" ' Not on your life ! ' I answered. ' I quit chasing you in Indiana when they let you go.'

" ' Don't give me away, Murray,' he pleaded. ' I blew all the money in six months.'

" ' I'm not going to give you away,' I said, ' but I am vexed still at that gaoler.'

" Mr. Finney had gone to bed, but I sat up until three o'clock in the morning with Flanders, while he told me of himself and of crooks he had known.

" ' You did wrong to accuse the gaoler,' he said. ' He did not let me go.'

" I went away the next day, and I lost track of Flanders. Along towards 1888 I was with old John Klippert at Berlin, when none other than J. O. Flanders stepped off the train.

" ' John,' said I to Klippert, ' tell that polite, fine gentleman over there that his presence is desired in the United States.'

" Old John walked over and thumped Flanders on the shoulder.

" ' You're vanted in t'e States, und vanted quick,' said old John.

" ' Thank you, my deah fellah, I know it well,' said Flanders.

" Old John gasped. He hastened back to me and exclaimed :

" ' He admits it, Shon ; he admits it ! Vill I jigger him ? Say t'e vord, Shon, und I got him.'

" Flanders spied me and promptly came over and bowed. I explained to him that I had changed positions since seeing him in London, and perhaps, if he still contemplated the easy, anxious life, it would be better for him to sojourn in the States. He understood, bowed politely, thanked me for past courtesies, and took the waiting train out of Berlin again. Old John gazed after him.

" ' He looked a shentleman, but I could tell he vas a horse thiever,' said old John, and he chuckled, then looked at me and said, ' I can tell 'em efery time, t'e horse thievers, Shon,' and he shook his old head wisely.

" I never saw Flanders again."

144

25

TWO DISAPPEARANCES

In the united counties of Stormont, Dundas, and Glengarry, where Louis Kipp served a year for his part in the big circus fight, the county treasurer was Aeneas Macdonald. He held office as a nominee of the Government. He was one of the leading men of that part of the country, active in business and social affairs, and of a prominent and influential family.

" Aeneas was married, and was about forty years old," says Murray. " He was popular, and knew everybody in the three counties. One evening he was rowing on the St. Lawrence River, opposite Cornwall. He was seen at sunset in the boat. When he did not return his wife became alarmed and a searching party was organised. The boat was found, capsized and floating aimlessly about in a little bay, and later his hat was found in the water. The river was dragged, and men dived for the body, but it could not be found. Mrs. Macdonald put on widow's weeds. Aeneas was mourned as lost. Several bodies, found at various points along the river, were held in the belief that one of them might be the missing man, but none was identified as Macdonald. He had been county treasurer for many years, and his death occasioned widespread sorrow. It was thought at first that a stranger had been with him in the boat, and that he might have met with foul play, and, as in the Long Point or Piggott case, the body would wash loose from the weights attached to it and rise to the surface. Those who last saw Aeneas in the boat were confident he was alone and beyond the reach of any one seeking his life. Suicide was scouted. Aeneas loved life too well for that.

" A new county treasurer, Mr. Mathias, who died recently,

was appointed, and Aeneas passed into the history of the three counties as an honest man and an upright official, who had come to an untimely end by accidental drowning. Months passed. The last hopes of finding the body were abandoned. Then the widow notified the insurance companies to pay to her the amount of her late husband's life insurance policies. It came to light then that Aeneas had taken out policies for thousands of dollars. The companies refused to pay until they had more positive proof of the death of Macdonald. They professed to believe he was alive and not dead. Mrs. Macdonald began an action against the insurance companies to get the money. In the meantime the new county treasurer had been verifying the accounts of the office, and he found that Macdonald had embezzled thousands of dollars from the county funds, and had committed forgery and other crimes.

"In the spring of 1888 the Government instructed me to find Macdonald. This action was due to the requests of the county officials of the united counties, and the letters of the officers of the insurance companies. It was a hard case. I sent personal communications to my police friends throughout the continent. The search was conducted largely in a confidential way, for I did not wish to arouse the suspicions of his friends, and he had many of them. I explained the circumstances of his disappearance in detail, and cautioned them to make sure of their man as a mistaken arrest would be unpleasant. About this time a body was found far down the St. Lawrence, and some who saw it said it was the body of Macdonald. The people of the united counties were divided as to whether Aeneas was living or dead. As time passed there were folk who asserted positively they had seen him drown.

"From police friends in California I heard of a man named Abner Holt, who, they thought, was Macdonald, if Macdonald were alive. Mr. Holt did not tarry long in California, but shortly thereafter, I heard of a James B. Carter, in Oregon, who was suspiciously similar to Abner Holt of California in appearance. Then I heard from police friends in Colorado of the arrival of a Walter Holder in Denver, and Mr. Holder

146

was a counterpart of Mr. Carter of Oregon, and Mr. Holt of California, and all three bore more or less resemblance to the ghost of Aeneas Macdonald. Next I heard of a Thomas Collier in St. Louis, and he, too, joined the list of duplicates of the missing Aeneas. These mysterious strangers popped up at intervals that satisfied me one man was travelling through the western part of the United States, with a change of names between cities. I determined to shake hands with this gentleman, and give him greetings in the name of those solicitous of the whereabouts of Aeneas.

" I prepared the necessary papers, properly authenticated, and at the next city where this travelling mystery appeared I hastened to take the trail. I fell in behind him in Omaha, from whence he had bought tickets to St. Paul, and with a glad heart I took the next train to see my old friends in Minnesota. Mr. Many Names was there ahead of me, and was running short of funds. In fact, the first trace of him I obtained was as an applicant for a job as a street car conductor. He was to return the next morning. When he appeared I was there.

" ' Good morning, Aeneas,' said I, shaking hands heartily. ' When did you get out of the river ? '

" ' I never got in,' said he.

" I took him before United States Commissioner Spencer on June 2nd. He was remanded until June 15th, and then until June 21st. In this interval a number of telegrams came to me from Cornwall and Toronto to drop the case. I refused to have Aeneas discharged, and I ignored the telegrams. Immediately after his arrest Aeneas had sent word to his friends in Canada. Finally I received a written communication from the then Deputy-Attorney-General to drop the proceedings. It was a matter of great surprise and disappointment to me and to the United States authorities that, with such a clear case against Macdonald, it should have been dropped. It is entirely unusual to drop such extradition proceedings. It was brought about no doubt by the refunding of some of the stolen money to the county officials and by the abandonment, of course, of the actions against the insurance companies. That is the only way I can account for such unprecedented instructions to drop extradition proceedings when the prisoner was before the United States Commissioner. I think it was a great miscarriage of justice.

"Aeneas Macdonald was released in St. Paul and the proceedings for his extradition were abandoned. He still is absent from Canada, and he never has returned. There are a few folk who possibly still cling to the belief that Aeneas was drowned, and that the man arrested was his double or his reincarnated spirit. But there are not many who think this. All others in the united counties know that Aeneas Macdonald was not drowned, and that he was apprehended later in St. Paul, Minnesota, and he would have been brought back but for the action of the then Deputy-Attorney-General in directing that the extradition proceedings be discontinued.

"Aeneas was inclined to piety at times. That may account for the happenings in which he was dead and was live again, was lost and was found.

"A few weeks after my return from St. Paul and Aeneas, there was another disappearance. It occurred hundreds of miles from the old home of Aeneas. About five miles from Thessalon, on the shore of Georgian Bay in the district of Manitoulin, lived a family of farmers named Gillespie. There was a pretty thirteen-year-old daughter, Maud Gillespie. Early in August 1888 she went out to pick berries and did not return. She was seen last near a trout stream, and a bully good trout stream it is, as I happen to know. Searching parties went out and hunted for days, but could find no trace of the child. On August 11th I went up to Thessalon and began another search. I organised parties and apportioned the territory, and sent some on foot and others in boats, and for days and nights we scoured the islands and the shores of Georgian Bay. We visited scores of Indian camps, and pushed on into the wilds, but could not find her. I knew she had no life insurance, and was not a county treasurer, and that her disappearance therefore was not suspicious, so far as she was concerned. Her parents were well-nigh distracted, and I determined to make a final effort to find her. With a small party I went far up to remote Indian camps, and in one of them I found an old squaw, who nodded and grunted to me, and I went outside with her.

"'White girl?' she asked.

"I nodded. The old squaw held out her hand.

"'Give,' she grunted. 'Give.'

"I drew out some money. She sniffed. I felt in my pockets. I had a couple of trout flies in some tinfoil; I took them out. The old squaw seized the glittering tinfoil eagerly, taking my last trout flies with it. She tucked it in her jet black hair, coarse as a horse's tail.

"'Me—see—white girl,' she muttered slowly. 'She go—so—so—so—,' and she waved far north with her long arm.

"'Alone?' I asked. 'She go alone? Indian take white girl?'

"But the old squaw only grunted and played with the tinfoil and trout flies in her hair. We searched farther north, and twice we heard from Indians of a white girl who had passed that way. When further trailing was hopeless we turned back and made our way to Thessalon. It was a long, hard tramp. On the fourth day I came to the trout stream, where the little girl last was seen. I was tired, and I stretched full length on the ground and idly gazed at the blue sky through the trees, and then rolled over and stared at the water. It was a lovely stream. It glided beneath the over-growth into a broad, deep pool, on whose placid surface the reflection of the waving trees rose and fell amid patches of mirrored blue. Farther down the stream narrowed and rippled over rocks, splashing and gurgling as it went. But there must be no drifting aside into a fish story. I lolled by the stream until my men came up, and we moved on. No further trace of little Maud Gillespie was found, and I returned to Toronto. Fifteen years passed. In May 1903 a surveying party was exploring in New Ontario north of Lake Superior, over four hundred miles from the Gillespie home. They came upon a white woman living with the Indians in the wilderness. She was the wife of a big chief. She possessed a rare beauty of the wilds, yet was not wholly like her associates. She lived as an Indian, and exposure had tanned her a deep, dark brown. At first she was unable to talk with the white men, then gradually her power of speech in English returned until she could talk brokenly and remember a few

English words. She finally recalled her name, Maud Gillespie, and her mother. They asked her if she wished to go back to her mother. She said she did, and they communicated with her people and she went back to them, a woman almost thirty years old. She had gone away a little girl of thirteen, fond of her mother, and constantly talking or singing in her childish way. She returned a silent, reserved woman, with the habits and manner and speech of an Indian. She had lost her language, she had become an Indian. Gradually her people are winning her back. It is like taming a wild creature, but eventually the inborn instincts will assert themselves, and much of the Indian life will fall away. They have been teaching her to speak her own language again, and she readily learned anew the songs she sang as a little child.

"This loss of language is a singular thing. I met an Englishman in South America who had lost his language, and he was distressed almost to distraction because of it. I have seen other cases, too, passing strange."

26

THE HOLLOWED CHOCOLATE

A CALL to Galt awaited Murray on his return from Thessalon and the search for Maud Gillespie. Great excitement prevailed in the county of Waterloo. Many people were terrified; others were infuriated. A fiend was among them spreading death and planning the extermination of whole families. No one had any clue to the mysterious one's identity. It might be a stranger, it might be a neighbour; it might be a person of high estate or it might be a creature of low degree. None knew, and there were myriad suspicions. It was as if an avenging angel or a deadly devil were abroad in the county, lurking to slay and escape unseen, leaving no trace of the manner of death. A victim arose in the morning well and happy, and fell lifeless before noon without a sign of sickness or an intimation of the end.

" The climax came when little Meta Cherry, the three-year-old daughter of John Cherry, a prominent mill-owner of Galt, died in a sudden and mysterious way," says Murray. " I went to Galt, a prosperous town near Berlin, in the county of Waterloo. It was September 1888. Several persons were sick, as if a plague were upon them. I looked at the little child. She seemed startled, even in death, as if the hand that thrust her into eternity had seized her roughly and scared her. I talked with John Cherry, and he told me of a box of chocolate drops that had come through the mail. He showed me the box. A few of the chocolates were gone. Meta had eaten them. I took one out, and carefully scraped the chocolate off with a knife-blade. I found on the bottom of the chocolate a spot where a cavity had been bored, and this had been filled with a whitish substance, unlike the cream candy of the chocolate, and the hole then had been sealed deftly by glazing over the bottom with more chocolate. I took the contents of the box, and sent the chocolates to Professor Ellis for analysis.

"I examined the box minutely. It revealed no clue, simply an ordinary pasteboard box. The wrapper in which it came showed a label pasted over an old address. The address on this label was printed with a soft lead pencil. I steamed the label to get at the address underneath it, but it had been washed out and scraped away, except for the one word 'Miss.' The package had been mailed in Galt. On inquiry I learned that similar packages had been received by the Rev. John Ridley, minister of the Church of England in Galt, and by Miss May Lowell and Mrs. Lowell, daughter and wife of Charles Lowell, proprietor of the Queen's Hotel in Galt. The boxes were quite small, and the inscriptions were alike as to the soft lead pencil. The packages had been dropped in the mail when no one was around, and the sender had vanished unseen.

"Professor Ellis reported that the cavities in the chocolate drops were filled with strychnine. This established clearly the intent of the poisoner to kill many people, and wipe out a number of families.

"I spent days gathering all the gossip of the town for generations back, hearing all the tales of trouble, and searching for some secret feud or some deadly hatred that would supply a motive for the deed. I ransacked ancestral closets for family skeletons, and I poked in all the after-dark affairs and twilight scandals since the days when the oldest inhabitants were gay young folk, fond of walking hand-in-hand through the gloaming. I ran down secrets that distressed dear old ladies, and left them in tears. I heard confessions of errors of youth that had lain locked in gentle bosoms for many kindly years; in fact, for a time I was an old Paul Pry Gadabout, poking my nose into other folk's business, until I felt I had sifted the lives and winnowed the chaff from the wheat in the collective career of the entire community. Every town has its chamber of horrors, where the sad episodes of indiscreet living are laid away to crumble in darkness, and the town of Galt has no more than its share of secrets of the passing generations. I found nothing in the long-gone years to throw light on the crime. There was no venerable hatred sufficient to inspire the murder of a little child. So I turned to later years, and for entanglements of recent months.

"In the meantime, about the middle of October, I arrested Hannah Boyd at Thorold. Hannah was a fine-looking girl, and had been living as a domestic in the Queen's Hotel, of which Mr. Lowell was proprietor. Later she removed to Thorold, and worked for a family there as Hannah Bond. Her home was in Hamilton. I kept her a week, and interviewed her thoroughly, particularly as to the family life of the Lowells, and whether she knew of the receipt of the package of chocolates by Mrs. Lowell and Miss Lowell, and whether she ever had heard of any trouble with the Ridleys, the Cherrys, and the Lowells. I was satisfied after these interviews with Hannah that she had no guilty knowledge, and that she had nothing whatever to do with sending the packages.

"I did develop promptly a strong suspicion as to the person who did send the poison packages. I searched the drug-stores through Canada, and examined the poison-books in all of them, and went so far as to describe to some of the the druggists the person I suspected; but I found no clue that would hold in a trial as sufficient evidence to convict anybody. It is one of the most aggravating cases of my entire experience, yet I hold steadfast to my first impression."

27

THE FOOTMARK BY LANGFORD'S BED

OLD Dick Langford was a miser, and the pride of his life was a fine bay horse with a white spot on his nose. Old Dick was eighty years old and the horse was eight. They lived on Old Dick's farm in the county of Carleton, six miles from the town of Carp, ten miles from Stittsville, and thirty miles from Ottawa. Many a time the shrivelled old man and the spirited bay horse had done the distance to Ottawa in less than four hours. Old Dick's wife had left him twenty years before he got the bay horse. She had said Old Dick was a skinflint and a torturer, and she would not live in the same county with him. He chuckled and showed his solitary front tooth, and transferred his farm so that she could not claim a part of it. After his wife was gone, Old Dick tried to regain title to his farm, but the man to whom he had transferred it disappeared, so Old Dick bought the farm near Carp and settled down alone, with his bay horse with the white spot on his nose, and a few farm horses, cows, chickens, dogs, and four books.

"Old Dick's bay horse was stolen in 1889," says Murray, "and the old man raised a tremendous hullabaloo. About three months later the horse was recovered in Ottawa and Old Dick was happy. In the fall of 1890 the horse was stolen again. Old Dick declared he knew the thief, and the adjoining counties were placarded with the following:

'STOP HORSE THIEF!

'Stolen from Richard Langford, Lot 13, Concession 8, Township of Huntley, County Carleton, on Friday night, October 3rd, 1890, A DARK BROWN HORSE; age 8; height 16 to 17 hands; weight about 14 cwt.; black points, except white spot on nose and white hind feet. May have traded since. Arrest

154

'GEORGE GOODWIN,

'alias St. George, alias Brennan ; height, about 5 feet 8 or
9 inches ; age, about 24 ; fair complexion, small sandy
moustache, sandy hair, slim build and sharp features ;
grey clothes, and wore a cap when last seen.   Take charge
of any horse he may have and wire
'R. McGREGOR,
'County Constable,
'Almonte, Ont.'

" Old Dick spent his time driving about with other horses
searching for his bay horse, and declaring that the thief would
go to prison this time.   In December Old Dick ceased
driving about and locked himself up in his house and devoted
himself anew to his library of four books.   The favourite was
a 'History of the Siege of Londonderry and Defence of
Inniskillen.'   The other books were 'Meditations and Con-
templations,' by the Rev. James Hervey ; 'A Short Defence of
Old Religion against Certain Novelties, Recommended to the
People of Ireland' ;   and a big family Bible.   Old Dick
would open the 'History of the Siege,' and lay it on the table.
Then he would shout passages from it at the top of his voice
and toddle up and down the room in the throes of great
excitement over the deeds of the lads of Londonderry.
" On Saturday afternoon, December 6th, 1890, three weeks
after Birchall was hanged, neighbours passing to and from
the town of Carp could hear Old Dick, the miser, roaring
away over the 'Siege of Londonderry.'   His door was locked
and his windows were barred, but his voice could be heard
while he thumped with his cane and trod the kitchen floor, as
if leading a gallant charge.   Robert Clark, a neighbour,
whose house was in plain sight of the home of Old Dick, saw
a light in the house in the early evening and at nine o'clock,
when he looked out, Old Dick's house was dark, the light
was out and the old miser, as was his custom, was supposed
by Clark to have gone to bed.   About half-past ten that
night, as Clark was locking up for the night, he looked out
and saw Old Dick's house brightly lighted, something Old
Dick never did, because he deemed it extravagance.   It was
so unusual, that Clark was on the verge of going over to see

155

if all was well with the old man; but it was snowing and blowing, so he concluded to wait until the next morning. On Sunday Clark went over to Old Dick's. The house was locked. It was blowing heavily. Clark beat on the door, and when no answer came he went to the barn. Lying on the floor of the barn was Old Dick, sprawled out senseless, his head a mass of frozen blood. Clark shouted over to his own house and his family came and they bore the old miser to his house, forced in the door and endeavoured to revive him. The doctors were called and they worked over Old Dick, but he died, declaiming a passage from the ' History of the Siege of Londonderry,' and speaking no word as to the identity of his murderer.

" I arrived before the old man breathed his last. His head had been beaten by a blunt, heavy instrument. I searched the barn and found an iron pin, thirty-seven inches long and weighing ten pounds. Old Dick had used it as a pin to fasten the barn door, but white hairs and blood on it showed the murderer had used it as a club to beat Old Dick's head almost to a pulp. The doctors, who examined the wounds on Sunday, said that Old Dick had been beaten on Saturday, and had lain all night in the barn. I searched the house. I found the ' Siege of Londonderry ' open on the table, as the old man had left it. I found his bed had been disturbed and that some one had slept in it; a man, judging from the footmark, which was not Old Dick's. The footmark showed no shoe, but seemingly a thick, wet sock. The murderer, whoever he was, called Old Dick out from his house to the barn on Saturday evening, either by hailing him or threatening to steal a horse, and as Old Dick entered the barn the murderer smote him with the iron pin and left him for dead, then quietly went to the house and lighted the light seen at half-past ten by Clark, who had thought at once that something was wrong, or Old Dick would not waste candles or oil. After warming himself at the fire, the murderer calmly went to rest in Old Dick's bed, and slept serenely while Old Dick lay dying in the barn with his wounds freezing. On Sunday morning the murderer had gone his way in the blinding snowstorm that covered his tracks.

"I began the usual house-to-house questioning of everybody in that part of the county, and at the very outset I was reminded of Old Dick's stolen horse and his belief that he knew the thief. At every house I asked if they had seen George Goodwin recently. Goodwin was known in that locality as a loose character. He chopped wood and did odd jobs for farmers. I found a farmer who had seen him early on Saturday evening about a mile from Old Dick's. Goodwin at that time was walking toward the Langford farm. I found another farmer who saw him still nearer Old Dick's house. Later I found another who saw him on Sunday bound in the opposite direction, away from Old Dick's. I got a good description of Goodwin. He was twenty-four years old, five feet eight inches tall, weighed one hundred and forty-five pounds, and had sandy hair and a light sandy moustache. He was bow-legged, had watery eyes, was near-sighted, and a silent fellow, who seldom spoke unless spoken to. But what satisfied me was the description of his clothing given by the farmers who saw him. He wore a blue suit, a short, striped overcoat, an imitation of lambskin cap, and beef-skin moccasins. The moccasins settled it. They accounted for the footmark in Old Dick's bedroom as of a thick, wet, stained sock. I billed Goodwin for Old Dick's murder. He was known also as Brennan, St. George, Wilkins, and used still other names. He had relatives living near Ottawa, and I expected him to go to them before jumping to the United States. He had not robbed Old Dick, for I found his money.

"Goodwin did precisely as I expected. He sent to his relatives for money, while he hid near Ottawa. I had hunted him through December 1890, and January and February 1891, and in March I located him near Ottawa. His trial was set for the Spring Assizes. His relatives retained Dalton McCarthy to defend him. Justice McMahon presided, and the trial was postponed until the Fall Assizes at the request of the defence. In the interval, Goodwin got out on bail. He skipped the country and never came back. It was good riddance of bad rubbish.

"I wondered often whether the murderer enjoyed pleasant

dreams when he lay down and slept in his victim's bed. The prosecution's theory was, that Goodwin had killed Old Dick, not for robbery necessarily, but because Goodwin had stolen Old Dick's horse and Old Dick knew he did it, and was waiting to locate him in order to have him arrested and sent to prison. If our theory as to the murderer had been wrong, Goodwin would not have been apt to run away.

" I had good luck in the Goodwin case, as indeed I have had in almost all cases. But about this same time I had a case where luck seemed wholly against me—in fact, I laid it away as a hard luck case. It was toward the close of 1890. John Brothers was the man in the case. He manufactured agricultural implements in the town of Milton, in the county of Halton, about twenty miles west of Toronto. He took farmers' notes in part payment for implements. He became hard up, placed his genuine notes in the bank and added some forged notes to them. In due time the manager of the bank told him to take up the notes. Brothers went to his brother-in-law, Amos Darling, an honest farmer who had a nice home earned by hard work. He dumped the notes on to Darling, telling him they were a good thing, paying seven and eight per cent. interest. Darling went to the bank and took up the notes, giving the bank his own note for $5,000, or almost the value of his farm. Brothers promptly disappeared, and the bank induced Darling to exchange his note for a mortgage on his farm, and in the end he lost his farm. I billed Brothers all over the country.

" Through a letter he wrote from San Francisco, I located him there. He was working as a moulder in the Risdon foundry. I prepared extradition papers and started for San Francisco. While I was on my way west and before I arrived there, a friend of Brothers in Canada notified him of extradition papers having been issued, and Brothers disappeared the day before I alighted from a train in Frisco. I notified the police all over the country, and after waiting some days and hearing nothing, I returned to Toronto. My train was several hours late. I learned that Brothers had been arrested by the chief of police at El Paso, Texas, on the Mexican border. The chief had wired me to Toronto and the telegram had been repeated to San Francisco and I was on my way back, so it missed me. I telegraphed immediately to El Paso, and the chief replied he had held Brothers as long as he could and had been compelled to release him a few hours before my telegram arrived, and Brothers had just left the town. If my train had not been late I could have reached the chief in El Paso in time. But luck was against me clear through in this case.

"Brothers crossed into Mexico and stayed there. I have heard he is dead. I felt very sorry for his brother-in-law, Amos Darling, whose home paid the forgeries of Brothers. Such Brothers as this one are not desirable even as brothers-in-law."

28

THE LADY OF THE PIERCING BLACK EYES

THE lady of the piercing black eyes crossed Murray's path in 1891. She was an amazon, and Murray avers she was a virago as well. Her maiden name was Nettie Slack, and her cradle was rocked in the county of Perth. As a young girl she was famed for her jet-black eyes and raven-black hair, the eyes as shiny as the hair was glossy.

"She grew to superb womanhood," says Murray. "She was very tall, very muscular, with big, broad shoulders and swinging tread, and the mien of a powerful man. Her piercing black eyes were wicked looking, and there were few men in the county of Perth who ventured to cross humours with Nettie Slack. She was rather a good-looking woman. Her eyes enhanced her attractiveness and yet seemed to mar her beauty. This may seem a paradox, yet in the case of Nettie Slack it was perfectly true. She was one of those big, sturdy, almost burly, women who remind you of re-incarnated creatures of ancient times, as if some of the white statues had turned to flesh and blood, with jet black tresses and adornings. As I looked at her the first time, I thought, 'What a ploughman you would make! What a woodman you would be!'

"She married. Her husband was her cousin, Thomas Blake Carruthers, a quiet, inoffensive young man, a prosperous farmer, who lived near St. Mary's, in the county of Perth. Nettie Slack was not exactly quiet, and in other ways she differed from her husband. They had two children, and Tom Carruthers was a good father. He managed his stalwart wife, too, and all seemed serene on the Carruthers' farm. One day old Grandpa Fotheringham, who was rich and lived in the township of Blanchard, county of Perth, died and left a goodly sum to his grandson, young Fotheringham, who knew Nettie Slack, and had gazed into her piercing black eyes. Young Fotheringham called on Nettie Slack after her marriage, and, of course, the gossips had their busy buzzings over the woman with the piercing black eyes and the man with his grandfather's money. I could have pictured Nettie Slack, if she had heard this gossip, sallying forth with a flail and belabouring the backs of all the busybodies. The reports of alleged improprieties between Nettie Slack and young Fotheringham continued, and finally Tom Carruthers was said to have twitted his wife about it, while she flamed in fury, with her jet-black eyes ablaze.

"Young Fotheringham took his money and went up on the Rainy River, in the wilds of the western part of this Province, and started a saw-mill. Then he returned to the county of Perth and saw Tom Blake Carruthers and told him that on the Rainy River was the place to live, with the money flowing in. Fotheringham induced Carruthers to sell his farm and move out to the Rainy River and build a house and work in the saw-mill. Nettie Slack Carruthers and the two little children, one four and the other two years old, accompanied Tom. They built a house near the mill and Carruthers worked in the mill. Nettie Slack kept house for Tom, and assisted a Mrs. Walt in the care of Fotheringham's home. Mrs. Walt said Nettie Slack was more like a visitor than a housekeeper. Fotheringham was unmarried. These conditions continued until January 1891. On the morning of January 3rd two shots resounded, and Nettie Slack rushed out of her house, shouting : ' Tom is dead ! Tom is dead !' She wrung her hands, and told those who came running to the house that she was down at the river after a pail of water when she heard the shots and ran up and found her husband dead on the floor. She had left him writing at a table. She was the principal witness at the inquest, and the coroner's jury brought in an open verdict.

"It was over two hundred miles to civilisation. There were no roads ; only a dog trail in winter. But after the inquest Nettie Slack took her two children and started out with the mail carrier to get away from Rainy River. She slept out four nights in the snowbanks, and finally arrived at Rat Portage, where she took the train for her old home near St. Mary's, in the county of Perth. After navigation opened in the spring, people in the Rainy River district began to talk, and in July 1891 I went up to Rainy River. I had the body of Tom Carruthers exhumed and a post mortem made, and had the head cut off. The moment I saw where the two bullets entered the skull I knew it was not suicide but murder. One had entered well around at the back of the head, behind the right ear. The other entered the left temple. The doctor showed that either would have caused death as it crashed into the brain, and I saw clearly that Tom Carruthers never shot himself in the back of the head, behind the right ear, and also in the left temple.

"Nettie Slack had said her husband had written a note of farewell as he sat at the table while she was out after a pail of water. I obtained this note. It read :

"'I was heartbroken and tired of life and decided to end the awful conflict. Good-bye.

'TOM.'

"I obtained specimens of Nettie Slack's handwriting. It was just as I suspected. The farewell note was a clumsy forgery written by her. I had this note photographed. I got the 38 calibre revolver. Tom was supposed to have written the farewell and then to have shot himself twice in the head and to have fallen dead on the floor beside the table. He fell dead, but the shots were fired by another. I returned to Rat Portage and laid an information against Nettie Slack Carruthers, and obtained a warrant for her arrest. I was on my way to St. Mary's when I learned she was in Toronto, and I arrested Nettie Slack Carruthers at the house of a Mrs. Walsh, and took her back to Rat Portage and locked her up. Her brothers were well-to-do, and they went to Rat Portage and saw her, and then engaged B. B. Osler, the foremost counsel in Canada, to defend her. The preliminary examination extended over a week, and Mrs. Carruthers was committed to the Port Arthur gaol for trial. All concerned knew a big legal battle would follow.

"I talked with the five-year-old child.

"'Popy shot himself; Popy shot himself,' the tot would repeat over and over.

"'Who told you to say that?' I asked.

"'Mammy,' said the child, and it began afresh, 'Popy shot himself; Popy shot himself.'

"Justice Armour presided at the trial. R. C. Clute prosecuted, and B. B. Osler defended. The trial did not come on until June 1892. In the meantime, Nettie Slack's sister, a nice-looking girl, had gone to Port Arthur and stayed at the house of a merchant. Nettie Slack, in her girlhood, had played the organ in the country church near St. Mary's, and her sister had an organ sent to the gaol and Nettie Slack played sacred music and sang hymns day after day. The men for jurors were selected by the sheriff and through some mistake the merchant, at whose house Nettie Slack's sister stayed, was drawn as a juror along with others inclined to be friendly to the prisoner.

"I had handwriting experts to prove the farewell note a forgery. The wily Osler admitted the letter was a forgery, and turning to the jury he exclaimed: 'What would a poor woman do in a strange country but look for an excuse to defend herself from an unjust accusation that might be made?' He was a great lawyer and a resourceful advocate, was Osler. I produced the skull and showed to the jury how impossible it was for Carruthers to have shot himself where the two bullets entered the head. Dr. Macdonnell had the skull in charge and it slipped and fell on the table and rolled to the floor. Nettie Slack laughed. Osler saw her, and quick as a flash he opened out his long gown like a curtain and stood so that the jury could not see her. Then he walked back to the box with his gown open and said:

"'You villain! It's crying you should be instead of laughing! You deserve to be hung!'

"I heard him. Straightway Nettie Slack wept.

"'That's better,' said Osler, and he drew in his gown.

"Osler and I often talked of this afterwards.

"One of the witnesses was a woodman, named Cameron. He stumbled and mumbled and hesitated in his testimony, evidently having a wholesome regard for Nettie Slack's powerful physique. The virago eyed him. Mr. Clute asked Cameron if Mrs. Carruthers had shown any signs of grief over her dead husband.

" ' I—I—well,' mumbled the reluctant Cameron, ' I don't think so.'

Up spoke the woman.

" ' Say yes, Cameron,' she said. ' You know you saw me kissing the body.'

" I proved where a spot of blood, some distance from the table and the body, had been washed up, but not sufficiently to obliterate the traces of it. I showed the woman was a clever shot with the pistol. I showed that Fotheringham was not near the house at the time, and that no one but Tom and the woman and the two tots were there. Tom and the tots could not have done the shooting. The charge of Justice Armour emphasised this and clearly indicated who was guilty. The jury had a hard tussle, but the friends stood fast. Mrs. Carruthers was acquitted on Saturday, June 11th, 1892. She came down from Port Arthur on the same boat I did. She spied me on deck and came over to me.

" ' Well, Murray, you didn't hang me after all,' she said.

" ' I don't hang anybody,' said I.

" She looked at me and smiled.

" ' You were pretty decent,' she said, ' but that old rowdedow of a judge tried to put the black cap on me right in court.'

" After the verdict Justice Armour had said to the jurors that their verdict was not consistent with the evidence, and had said to the woman : ' Prisoner, you are acquitted ; I hope your conscience is acquitted.' The woman sneered.

" ' Murray, life's sweet, but it isn't worth much without liberty,' she said, as she sniffed the air aboard boat, after almost a year in gaol.

" I watched her as she stood there, her eyes flashing, her bosom heaving, a towering creature stirred by a sight of water, land, and sky.

" ' Murray,' she said, suddenly, tensely, ' it was worth it.'

" ' What was worth what ? ' I said.

" She laughed ; then her face, for once, seemed to become almost sad.

" ' I mean the year in gaol,' she said. ' A whole year out of my life.'

" She looked full at me, then walked away. It was my last glimpse of the lady with the piercing black eyes."

29

AN ESCAPER OF GENIUS

A MAN of many disguises appeared in Canada in 1890. He had wigs and beards and moustaches of varying sizes, shades, and shapes. He had a walk and talk, and complete change of clothes to match every alteration of hair and face Sometimes he was a French tourist, again a patriarchal clergyman, again a gruff, bluff Englishman, then a keen Yankee trader, next a quiet country gentleman, then a prosperous American banker, next an innocent old farmer, until he seemed to have stepped out of the pages of fiction, a remarkable character who would flit around a corner—and, presto! he was a different man.

"His first appearance was in Halifax, Nova Scotia," says Murray. "He purported to be a yachtsman, and put up at the best hotel, registering as Mr. Thompson. He stayed a few days, getting acquainted quickly, and saying he expected his yacht to arrive shortly, and he had come on from Boston by rail. He looked the typical gentleman yachtsman. Finally he went to a wholesale liquor and supply house and bought $500 worth of wines and groceries for his yacht, to be delivered aboard on the yacht's arrival. He presented a Boston draft for $2,000, and they accommodatingly gave him $1,500 cash. He skipped. His next stop was at Moncton, one hundred and fifty miles north of Halifax, where he appeared as a gay young sport, expecting some horses to arrive. He finally got into the hotel for $500 on a bogus draft, and then flitted to the eastern townships of the Province of Quebec, where he did a land office business in drafts, and where he posed as a minister, a doctor, and a German globetrotter. He seemed to have some hypnotic power over the hotel people and tradesmen. They cashed his bogus drafts without suspicion. From Quebec he jumped to Belleville, Ontario, where he bought a suit of clothes from a merchant

165

tailor about noon on a Saturday, shortly before the banks closed. He gave the tailor a draft for $500, the tailor endorsed it, the bank cashed it, and away went the stranger. He skipped Toronto, and alighted in Listowell. There he pretended to be buying horses, and he did buy a horse. A man named Laurie met him there.

"There was a private banker in Listowell named John Scott, who was very rich and very close. He had a fine fancy team. The stranger offered to buy the team from Scott. They had two or three dickers over it. In the course of one of these horse talks the horse-buyer asked Scott what discount he charged on American drafts. Scott named a rate. The stranger said it was too much.

"'I don't want to pay that much,' he said. 'I've got them cashed at so-and-so, and so-and-so, and so-and-so, for less,' he added, naming a number of places and banks and bankers.

"At length he made an arrangement with Scott to cash a draft on the First National Bank of Mahanoy City, Pennsylvania, William L. Yoder, cashier, for $1,000. He got the money and skipped out. Scott was furious.

"The next place this draftsman turned up was in Winnipeg. It was here he showed his first sign of drink. He had gone through Canada from the Atlantic Ocean on the east, cashing bogus drafts totalling high up in the thousands, without a slip-up, and he was well on his way toward the Pacific Ocean, when he stopped in Winnipeg and got a jag. He went to a bank to get a draft for $1,000 cashed on a Louisiana bank. Like all his drafts the handiwork was perfect. But his leering manner aroused the suspicions of the manager of the bank, who told him to leave the draft 'until the manager comes in,' and to return in three hours, and see the manager, who would cash it for him. The manager played it well, although if the stranger had not been drinking he would not have returned. The manager telegraphed to the Louisiana bank, and the answer came that the draft was bogus. The stranger, who was going under the name of Hale in Winnipeg, called again at the bank after three hours, was arrested, convicted of attempting to pass bogus drafts, and sent to gaol for one year as Edward Hale.

166

" I got after him in 1892. Some of those he fleeced held back for months before they notified any one of it. I started after him on the Scott case, and all the while he was in gaol in Winnipeg. I finally located him there. He heard I was after him, and he became very religious in the gaol, and at length he preached there to his fellow prisoners, exhorting them to reform and forsake evil ways. Crossley and Hunter, the evangelists, went to see him, and heard him preach, and thought he was reformed. The Rev. Mr. Crossley wrote to the Attorney-General and to me about him. I read the letter, and laid it away. I was biding my time, waiting for the expiration of Hale's time in Winnipeg. The day he walked out of gaol I intended to take him to Ontario to answer for the Listowel draft.

" Hale sent for Fighting MacKenzie, who had acted as attorney for Dobbin on one of my visits to Winnipeg.

" There is $1,000,000 in it if I can get out,' said Hale. 'I was full when I did this, and I never did it before. If I can get free it means millions.'

" Hale then told of a patent he had for 'manufacturing mosaic embroidery.' He sent for his wife, who came from the States, bringing a working model of this patent. Hale produced also forged patent rights for the United States and Canada, such clever forgeries that the lawyer did not detect them.

" ' I'll give you half the patent rights if you give me $1,500,' said Hale. 'It is worth $200,000 to anybody, but I want to get out. If I was out I would not take $200,000 for a quarter interest in it.'

" The turnkey was called in. He agreed to give $500 for half the Canada patent rights. The attorney was to give $1,000 for half the United States patent rights. The $1,500 was paid to Hale, who gave it to his wife, and she went away, taking the cash with her. The patent papers were executed. Consul Taylor was called in and witnessed the transaction.

" Then came the question of Hale's release. He explained that he must have his liberty to realise on the patents. In telling later of what happened he said the turnkey took a saw to his cell.

167

"'Saw the bars and get out, so I may keep my skirts clear,' he said.

"Hale went down with the saw and returned almost immediately.

"'That won't saw hard butter,' said Hale, and he threw down the saw in disgust.

"That night he was let out into the open yard. He returned to the window and hailed the turnkey.

"'How do I get over the wall?' asked Hale.

"'There is a loose board walk a foot wide,' said the turnkey 'Put it over the wall and slide down.'

"This is Hale's story. He did as he said the turnkey told him. He left a note stating nobody was to blame, and telling how he was supposed to have escaped. The escape was reported, and I set out to get Hale. With his disguises off he was a little, smooth-shaven, sandy-haired fellow, with false front teeth. I had his photograph, which had been taken as he was, without make-up or disguise, when he was locked up in Winnipeg. I knew he was a clever man. His work proved him to be as shrewd as any crook on the continent. I went to New York and saw Byrnes, and some of his officers remembered him. He had hung out in Brooklyn, and was known as Ed. Hayes. Those who knew him said he was as slick in his line as any man in America. I went to Winnipeg, and learned there that when the model of the supposed patented machine had arrived in Winnipeg with Hale's wife, it had been shipped by express from St. Paul, Minnesota. I had learned in New York that Hale's name was Ed. Failing. I prepared extradition papers, and went to Minneapolis, arriving there on Wednesday, April 11th, 1892. I conferred with my old friend, Jim Hankinson, for thirty years a detective. We began a hunt for people of the name of Failing, and we found the superintendent of the cattle yards near New Brighton was named Failing, and was a prominent and influential man. From neighbours of his we learned he had a brother, Ed. Failing. A liveryman at New Brighton, who was a friend of Hankinson, knew Ed., and said he was living in a secluded, lonely place some miles out of New Brighton, with his wife and two children. The liveryman said he came in for his mail about three times a week at eight o'clock in the morning. We waited, and on the second day he drove up to the post office. I arrested him.

"He became greatly excited, shouted that it was an outrage, and declared I had the wrong man, and that he was an honest farmer. He ranted while I snapped the handcuffs on him, and then he quieted down, still protesting it was a mistake, and asked to be permitted to go out to his home and say good-bye to his folks. I consented, and we drove out to his home. His wife greeted us at the door—a red-haired, pretty young woman of twenty-five. She nodded indoors, and an older, grey-haired woman appeared. Failing said she was his mother. When Failing told them of his arrest and how I had consented to let him say good-bye to them, one of them fell on my neck to embrace me. I pretended not to feel her hand slip into my pockets hunting for the key to the the handcuffs, but I stepped back so quickly that her hand caught. I extricated it, and apologised for the clumsiness of my pocket and its rudeness in holding her hand.

"Failing started to walk through the house. He explained that he wanted to bid the old place good-bye. I bade him keep in my sight and not far from me.

"'I don't intend to have you mistaking me for the old place, and bidding us both good-bye,' said I.

"He appeared much hurt, and said I spoke harshly to one who was an innocent farmer. We drove to St. Paul, leaving his family weeping in the doorway until they thought we were out of sight, but a bend in the road showed them without trace of tears. Failing fought extradition. He denied being in Canada, and he called several witnesses to prove an alibi. I had gone east and arranged for my witnesses from Canada. On my trip east, I met my old friend Chief Cusack, of Buffalo, on the train, and we had a pleasant ride together, and exchanged some photographs of crooks, and among those he gave me was the picture of a fellow who, with Shell Hamilton, had been arrested some time before in Buffalo for attempting a sneak on Mrs. Dickinson's jewellery store. I had seen the pair at the Buffalo police headquarters, and had looked them over. I had the photographs with me when I returned to St. Paul for the extradition proceedings.

"One of the witnesses called by Failing to prove an alibi was a young man named Collins. He was the last called, following the wife, the mother, and a tailor and other friends, who swore Failing was in Minneapolis the day he foisted the bogus draft on Banker Scott at Listowel, in Canada. Collins swore he was with Failing in Minneapolis all that day, and that he (Collins) was connected with a Turkish bath in the West House. I pulled a photograph out of my pocket, and handed it to my attorney, Markham.

"'Were your ever in Buffalo, New York, Collins?'

"'No,' said he.

"'Ever know Shell Hamilton?'

"'No,' said he.

"'Is that your photograph?'—and Markham handed him the picture Cusack had given to me.

"Collins wavered, but blurted out: 'No.'

"I took the stand, and told of seeing Collins in a cell in Buffalo, and I showed the commissioner the police photograph. That settled the alibi. I had Bob Wood, a liveryman of Listowel, who identified Failing positively, and I had W. L. Yoder, cashier of the Mahanoy City bank, who swore the draft was a forgery. Commissioner Spencer committed Failing for extradition, and on May 16th I started for Listowel with the prisoner. He protested it was an outrage, and he was not the Failing I was after. Up to Stratford he denied his identity.

"'Well,' he said, as the train left Stratford. 'Listowel is next. I give up the ghost. I'll put you to no more trouble.'

"'I don't care a cuss whether you do or not,' I answered, tartly; for he had done all he could to block me, and ever was on the alert for an opportunity to escape.

"Then he told me all about the Winnipeg business, and the fake patent, and the getting out of gaol. Banker Scott was at Listowel when we arrived. When Failing saw him he walked up and seized the hand of the astonished Mr. Scott, and shook it heartily before the banker could draw it away.

" ' Well, well! How are you, Mr. Scott? How de do?' said Failing cordially.

" Banker Scott crimsoned with wrath, and snatched his hand free.

" ' Dang scoundrel! Rascallion! Villain! Blackguard!' sputtered Banker Scott. ' How dare you shake hands with me?'

" ' Between two gentlemen,' responded Failing airily.

" He was committed for trial, and I took him to Stratford gaol, and warned the gaoler that he was a slippery fellow. The gaoler was an old soldier, who grew indignant over the reminder. Failing greeted him suavely, and bade him not be wrathful at me, as I meant well. I laughed to myself. Failing was to be tried at the Fall Assizes. A few days before the Assizes were to begin I received a letter from him saying he would plead guilty, and he hoped I would put in a good word for him. The next day he escaped from Stratford gaol. As in Winnipeg, he left a note saying no one was to blame. He also left a wooden key he had made from a round of a chair. The key was nicely made, but I had my doubts about his unlocking four doors with that key. I received telegrams from the authorities about his escape, but I never made much of an effort to get him. I heard of him frequently thereafter for several years. He passed cheques in Salt Lake City, and escaped. He worked off some drafts in Ogden and escaped. I heard he beat gaol five times thereafter. He turned up in Carson City, Nevada, then in California, and later in Colorado. He was a clever one with the blarney, and was a great ' con ' man.

" Professionals considered him one of the cleverest in the business. He was a bird, but not a gaol-bird if he could help it, and he usually managed to help it. I suppose there are gaolers in both the United States and Canada who hold him in tender remembrance."

30

PENNYFATHER OF THE BANK

PENNYFEATHER'S life was one long series of additions and sub-
tractions. Pennyfeather was an accountant in the Chatham
branch of the Standard Bank. He was a faithful fellow, and
if $9,000 had not vanished from the Chatham branch, Penny-
feather to this day might have been adding columns of figures
and peering at depositors through the crosswork of his cage
in the bank.

"There was a township fair near Chatham on October 1st,
1892," says Murray. "The day after the fair it was found
that $9,000 in bills had disappeared from the bank. The
Department was notified immediately, and I went to Chatham.
I found the bank's safe untouched. It had not been forced,
and there had been no tampering with its locks. I examined
Manager Rogers. He knew nothing about it. The cash that
had vanished was in charge of Cashier Brown. I called in
Cashier Brown, and questioned him. He said he had put the
$9,000 in a tin box, and during business hours of the bank on
October 1st the tin box was out of the vault, as was customary
with a cashbox, and was in its usual place in the cage.
Cashier Brown said that, owing to his desire to get away to
the fair, he had closed the vault hurriedly and forgot to put
the cashbox in the vault. In fact, he had supposed it had
been put in the vault before he closed it.

"I went out and talked to the people across the street from
the bank, and asked them particularly about whether they had
seen any person in or around the bank after the bank closed.
Cashier Brown's statement had satisfied me that no burglars
had done the job, but some one aware of the fact that the tin
box full of cash had been left out of the vault must have had
a hand in it, if he was not the sole perpetrator of the crime.
A person to have this knowledge of the tin box must have

been in the bank when Cashier Brown closed the vault, or must have gone into the bank after it had been locked up for the day. No locks had been forced on any of the doors of the building. The people across the street had seen no strange persons in or around the bank after the usual time for closing the vault.

"I returned to the bank. Pennyfeather, the accountant, who had been out at luncheon, had returned, and I called him in. Pennyfeather came into the private room very slowly. He walked with a mincing tread, as if to avoid stepping on eggs. He had just been married. In fact, he had violated a rule of the bank, which forbade an employee getting married unless he was in receipt of a certain amount of salary from the bank. The object of this rule was to compel employees to incur no incumbrances beyond their resources, and a wife was regarded as an incumbrance ; and in his efforts to provide properly for her, the young husband, who married on insufficient income, might be tempted to borrow from the bank's funds. I have heard a variety of opinions expressed about this rule. Thirty years ago I knew folks who married on fifty cents and a horse and waggon, and some had nothing but hope and faith. They got along well, but of course they were not employed in a bank. It may be a wise rule, but when two young folks, with their full share of 'gumption,' decide that in the course of human events it was intended they should get married, all the banks in Christendom are not apt to avail. Marriages are made in heaven, not in banks, we are told. The compound interest of happiness or misery resulting from them may cause us to wonder if, after all, banking rules may not govern the transaction.

"Pennyfeather had broken the rules of the bank. He had married on a salary below the minimum fixed for wedding wages. He was to be discharged. He knew it some days before the tin box vanished. He knew that if he married he would lose his job with the bank. He knew also that it might be many a day in the bank before he could expect to reach the marriage sum in the salary line. So he decided to marry anyhow, on the theory that even if he did not work in a bank he would not have to get off the earth. Then he married, and then the $9,000 cash in the tin box disappeared. I looked at Pennyfeather, the happy young husband, and I smiled. Pennyfeather smiled a wan smile.

" ' 'Tis a pleasant day, Mr. Pennyfeather,' said I. ' Be seated.'

" Pennyfeather sat down. Instantly he arose.

" ' Excuse me a moment, please,' said he. ' I feel ill. I will return.'

" ' Thereupon Pennyfeather hastened to the toilet-room, and presently I heard a noise as of a man in the throes of retching. In a few minutes Pennyfeather returned, pale and faint, and sank into a chair. I had been in the toilet-room a few minutes before, to wash the grime from my hands after poking around in the vault. I knew there was no way of escape from it, for as I lathered my hands with a big cake of soap I had looked for outlets from the room.

" ' Now please tell me, Mr. Pennyfeather, the last you saw of this tin box and its contents,' said I.

" Pennyfeather gulped and gasped.

" ' Excuse me again, please,' said he, and he made a second hurried exit to the toilet-room, and once more I heard the noise of belching ; and presently in came Pennyfeather, pallid and feeble, with his voice quite weak.

" Pennyfeather dropped into the chair, and gazed at me with sunken eyes, and on his lips were little flecks of foam.

" ' Have you ever had fits, Mr. Pennyfeather ? ' I asked politely. ' I mean, to the best of your knowledge or recollection have you ever had fits ? '

" Pennyfeather closed his eyes and breathed heavily. I waited. Finally he opened them a wee bit and looked at me.

" ' You were about to say where you last saw the tin box and its contents,' I resumed.

" Up rose Pennyfeather again.

" ' Excuse me,' said he, ' I am seized again.'

" Away he went to the toilet-room. I noticed that he went with celerity, but returned with difficulty. I heard again the rumblings of a human volcano in a state of eruption. I waited, and at length Pennyfeather tottered in and collapsed in a chair. He was breathing like a fish out of water, and his lips were frothy.

174

" ' My dear Mr. Pennyfeather,' I began. ' Let us forget the interruptions, and begin anew with your last sight of the contents of the tin box.'

" But Pennyfeather staggered to the toilet, and when he reappeared he was ghastly white and deathly sick, judging from appearances.

" ' I must go home,' he whispered. ' I am purging and retching myself away. I feel death in me. I will see you when I recover, if I ever do recover.'

" I bowed, and Pennyfeather was escorted to his home, and two doctors were called in to attend him. After he had gone an idea struck me. I went to the toilet-room to wash my hands. I picked up the soap, and lo! instead of the big cake I had used before Pennyfeather came in, there was a mere remnant of what once had been the cake.

" ' Has some one eaten it ? ' I exclaimed to myself.

" That night I called at Pennyfeather's house with President Cowan of the Standard Bank. Pennyfeather seemingly was very ill, moaning faintly, and looking very white. His wife was there. President Cowan got Dr. Brown the next morning, and the physician examined Pennyfeather. All the doctors said he had typhoid fever.

" ' Can he be suffering from soapus typhus ? ' was my question.

" ' Might I ask what soapus typhus is ? ' asked one of the doctors.

" ' A state of collapse superinduced by over-indulgence in toilet soap,' I said.

" They held it was typhoid fever. I said that if he had typhoid it would be weeks before he was able to be out. I went away. When Pennyfeather got up from his sick bed, he was arrested by Officer McGee, of Windsor. He was tried and acquitted while I was out of the country. Of course he no longer worked for the bank. He became a tavern keeper.

" I never had any positive proof that Pennyfeather ate soap. I recall Clutch Donohue, in Kingston, who ate soap to break his health, and thereby gain a pardon. He ate too much, and after he got out he died in a hotel outside the penitentiary walls before he could get home."

31

THE GANGS OF BURTCH AND RUTLEDGE

THE mysteries of the codes of communication among inmates of penitentiaries are regarded by some as past finding out. To others they constitute simply a series of coughs, taps, footscrapes, and occasional whispers, all significant with some meaning or message understood by the other convicts who hear them. But the bulk of tangible communication is done by whispers, and the taps or coughs are chiefly the signals of the whereabouts of guards or keepers. Telegraphers who have served time have been known to have secret cipher codes, and in the night they chatted by gentle tapping or subdued coughing, each tap and cough equivalent to the tick of a telegraph instrument. Two telegraphers who worked in a stone yard, and later in a shop in a penitentiary talked all day long, the taps of their hammers answering for the click of the telegraph.

"In the latter part of 1894 a series of burglaries occurred in various parts of the Province, and from the outset I was satisfied the jobs were the work of professionals, and daring, desperate professionals, too," says Murray. "I was making my best endeavour to capture them, and early in the chase I learned that there were two gangs at work, and that both of them had been organised in Kingston before their members had finished the sentences they then were serving. There was not much difference in the dates of their discharge, and they took in some pals from outside when they began to work. Some of the early burglaries supplied witnesses, who gave me good descriptions of strangers seen near the places robbed shortly before the jobs were done. I thus was able to figure out the make-up of the two gangs.

"In one gang were Frank Rutledge, a highwayman and burglar; Billy Black, a safe breaker; Walter Irvine, a burglar;

and Lew Lawrence, an all-round man. In the second gang were old Jimmy Stull, a former telegrapher; Howard Burtch, who already had done several years in Illinois, apart from his Canada time; and Frank Jackson, a Cleveland crook, who was wanted in the States for murder, and who had served time after I had sent his father down for counterfeiting. They were a fine collection of clever, desperate crooks. Several of them had done murder in their time, and they cared little for human life. They had set out, evidently, to clean up a fortune by burglary in Canada. Job after job was pulled off. Sometimes there were two jobs in one night, both gangs being busy. I was able, by descriptions after the robberies, to trace each gang. I determined to break them up if I had to stay awake nights for a year. I sent out, very carefully, descriptions of the gangs to trusted friends in the States and in Canada. I also set a watch on the home of Rutledge. His father lived in Streetsville, Ontario.

"On November 2nd, 1894, I was informed that Rutledge's gang had arrived in Streetsville. I took Detectives Davis, Cuddy, and others, and went to Streetsville, arriving later that evening. We prepared for a stiff fight. We surrounded the Rutledge house, creeping up to it quietly. Then we burst in the doors and entered. The birds had flown. They had slipped out not a minute too soon. The table was spread, the coffee on it was still warm. We found Rutledge's father and mother. They, of course, said they knew nothing of the visit of their son and his gang. Yet they were unable to explain why the table was set for six, with food and coffee for six. We went to a second house, where a man named Bill Ward lived. Ward was a friend of the Rutledges, and also had done time. We cracked it open, but the gang had gone. I was chagrined considerably, as I had hoped to bag the Rutledge bunch, and I knew it would be many a day before they would turn up in Streetsville again after such a close call.

"A few nights later the banking house of Hartman & Wilgress, in Clarksburg, near Thornbury, in the county of Grey, was burglarised. The thieves made an effort to get into the safe, but they were foiled by circumstances, and

177

succeeded in getting into the outer vault only. In this outer vault, however, was a large quantity of valuable silver ware, wedding presents to Mr. and Mrs. Wilgress, also a number of exceedingly rare and high-priced coins owned by Mr. Hartman. The burglars stole all this silver ware and all the coins. I went to Thornbury the next day, and the descriptions of strangers seen near the town a few hours before the burglary showed that it was another job by my old friends, Irvine, Rutledge, and Black. I returned to Toronto, and laid plans to trace the silver ware.

"In due time Irvine walked into the back office of a jeweller in Toronto with a bar of silver and sold it. This bar had been made by melting the Wilgress wedding presents. Irvine also visited the Gladstone House in Toronto, and showed a rare Chinese coin to the bar-tender, and later gave the coin to him. We got Irvine in Toronto, and the jeweller and bar-tender identified him, and Mr. Hartman identified the coin. I took Irvine to Owen Sound, where he was convicted on Thursday, December 13th, 1894, and was sent to Kingston for five years. He was the first. Bud Kinney had been with Irvine and the gang in several of their jobs. Bud was shot dead at Port Dalhousie in a robbery attempted there. Black I got in Hamilton, caught red-handed. He got five years.

"Rutledge jumped the country. He crossed to the United States, and turned up in Greely County, Colorado, where he was arrested for stealing a bicycle. In his pocket they found clippings about Irvine and Black, and a slip with my name on it. The sheriff telegraphed to me, and I sent him Rutledge's history. At the trial of Rutledge, in Colorado, my letter to the sheriff was read. Rutledge was convicted and sent down for six years.

"'When I get out I am going back to Canada and kill that —— Murray!' Rutledge declared.

"In 1901 he reappeared in Canada at the head of another gang, and due notice came to me that Rutledge intended to kill me. His particular pal was a crook named Rice. They had a third bird with them. They were trailed on one of their first jobs, and were followed to Chicago, caught there, extradited and tried for the Markham burglary. They were being taken in a carriage from the court house to the Toronto gaol, when some one threw a package into the carriage. Constables Steward and Boyd were in the carriage with the prisoners. The package contained loaded revolvers. The prisoners grabbed the revolvers, and one of them shot and killed Boyd, who was a good officer. After the shooting the prisoners jumped out of the carriage, ran to a street car, and tried to take possession of the car. Constable Steward followed, and in the shooting one of the burglars was killed. Rutledge and Rice were re-captured, and were taken to gaol. Rutledge ran up to the third corridor of the gaol, leaped over the railing, turned a complete somersault, and landed on the stone floor beneath. He was killed by the fall, a case of suicide. Rice was hanged.

" Lew Lawrence was caught in 1894, and tried in Berlin for a burglary at Galt, where his identification was perfect. He was convicted, and went back to Kingston for seven years. So ended the first gang—Rutledge dead, Kinney dead, Irvine, Black, and Lawrence back in Kingston.

" The second gang was led by Howard Burtch. He was a desperate burglar. He had served three years here, then had gone to Chicago, where he shot and killed a policeman while committing a burglary. He was sent to Joliet Penitentiary in Illinois for twenty years, but later his lawyers enabled him to get out. He came back here, and after a series of burglaries I got a perfect case against him in St. Catharine's. Burtch skipped to the States, and I got him in Buffalo in 1896. He had been sent down for larceny there, and as he came out of the penitentiary I took him. He fought extradition, but I brought him back, and he got ten years. He is in Kingston Penitentiary now.

" Old Jimmy Stull, one of Burtch's pals, was a funny little fellow. Jimmy was past fifty, although he always was sensitive on the subject of his age. He had been a telegraph operator in earlier years, and never failed to give his occupation as 'a member of the profession of telegraphy.' When Jimmy was broke he would go to the nearest telegraph office, and tap with his finger a request for a loan. He usually got

179

it, too. Jimmy was slippery, and it was not until 1897 that I arrested him. I got him in June of that year. He made a wry face, and said he had hoped he never would set eyes on me in either this world or the next. The burglary for which he was tried was the robbery of James H. Goring's store in Wellandport. Jimmy was convicted at St. Catharine's, and went to Kingston for five years.

"Frank Jackson got away to the States. He bothered us no more over here. So ended the second gang. It took three years or more to tuck them all away, but in the end they were broken up. Out of the eight men, two were dead, five were back in prison, and one was in exile.

"'The exile is the worst off of all of us,' said old Jimmy Stull."

32

THE KILLING OF JAMES AGNEW

" WHEN I die I intend to die on my own land ; I frown on trespassing and I am agin trespassing corpses most of all."

James Agnew preached this text in his life and practised it in his death. He was a retired farmer, an estimable old man, who lived with his wife on the outskirts of the town of Lindsay, in the county of Victoria, sixty miles east of Toronto. He kept a horse and a cow, and delighted to potter around the stable and the garden as a reminder of his many active years on a farm.

"I want no lingering and I want no trespassing when I die," he declared.

On the night of March 11th, 1896, the old man stepped out of his house to go to the stable, as was his custom, to make sure his horse and cow were comfortable and secure. It was eleven o'clock, pitch dark, and blowing and snowing. He left his wife knitting by the kitchen fire. He stumbled through the storm to the stable door and opened it. As he fumbled with the latch, death stalked through the snow, a crouching, wary figure. It stole close up to the old man and raised a hand as if pointing a finger at his white hair. There was a flash, a report, muffled in the gale ; the old man tumbled forward and fell. The figure stooped over him, rolled him over and silently vanished across the field and down the road. The wife knitted placidly by the kitchen fire. The minutes passed. She paused in her knitting, glanced uneasily at the clock, listened, then resumed her knitting, with an eye still on the clock, and finally arose, threw open the kitchen door, and called :

" James ! "

There was no answer. She called thrice, and then, in alarm, ran out through the storm to the stable, and tripped

181

over her husband's body in the doorway. With a shriek she fled to the nearest neighbour, Shannon by name, and the Shannons returned with her and found the old man dead, with a bullet hole behind the ear.

"The murder was shrouded in mystery," says Murray. "I was at Whitby at the time, in the Alger insurance conspiracy case, and I started immediately for Lindsay. The railroads were blocked with snow. I road and drove and walked and finally arrived. I examined the premises and came upon a peculiar track in the snow. The same track was observed by a neighbour on the night of the shooting. It was the track of an old rubber which had something fastened on the sole that made a mark in the snow like a small, rectangular hole. This track led from the door of the stable It was lost at times beneath the marks of other feet, but I found it farther away from the stable and followed it. The trail led to the house of Henry Logie, and on Logie's premises it was imprinted clearly in the snow. I talked with Mr. Logie. He had no such boot or shoe or rubber. But he had a young fellow working for him named John Carney, a big, overgrown boy of eighteen. His effects at Logie's were searched and an old rubber was found with a strap attached. I took this rubber or overshoe and strapped it on, so that the buckle of the strap was on the sole, and I stepped into the snow. The imprint was a duplicate of the imprint at Agnew's and of the track leading from the scene of the tragedy to Logie's.

"The house of Carney's father was searched, and old man Agnew's watch was found in the cellar. The watch and a few dollars had been taken from the body when the old man was murdered. All his pockets had been rifled and his papers and his empty purse were found lying on the floor of the stable. In addition to the watch a revolver was found, in Carney's house, of the calibre of the bullet that had crashed into Agnew's head. The trigger of this revolver was missing. Miss Marron found the trigger at Logie's, where she lived, and it was among young Carney's effects.

"I talked with everybody around the place, and I learned from several persons that they had seen young Carney

182

down town in Lindsay about ten o'clock that night. I ascertained he was with his brother, Patrick Carney, and later with two young men named Harry Bush and Edward Roach. In fact these young men were together on the road leading past Agnew's. I found a man named Edward Burke, who had passed the Agnew house and who heard a shot ring out just after he passed. Roach testified at the inquiry that Carney had fired two shots in the air from his revolver near the Agnews, and that, after they were fired, Roach and Bush went home, leaving Carney in the road near the Agnew house.

"John Carney and his brother Patrick were arrested, and on Tuesday, March 31st, were committed for trial. The trial occurred at the Spring Assizes. Justice Street presided. The defence was conducted ably by John Barron, Q.C., now County Judge of Perth. John King, Q.C., prosecuted. Pat Carney proved an alibi. John Carney was convicted and was sentenced to be hanged. The sentence later was commuted to imprisonment for life.

"When I finished with the Carney murder I went abroad for a yachting trip with friends. I sailed on the *City of Rome* on Saturday, June 6th, 1896, for Glasgow. It was my first real holiday in twenty years and I was as tickled as a schoolboy. I landed in Glasgow on June 16th and went to Edinburgh, where I spent a few days with relatives and old friends. On June 20th I sailed on the yacht *Norway* from Leith with a party of old-time friends. We cruised along the north coast of Scotland to Aberdeen and thence over the German Ocean to Norway, and went up north as far as the Lofoden Islands. On the trip back we visited various places along the coast of Norway and Sweden. We stopped in Copenhagen on June 27th, and there I met a brother of Captain Salmers of the steamer *Maipo*, whom I met in the Aitken case in South America. On June 28th we sailed for Kiel, and on July 1st we arrived in Hamburg.

"From Germany I went to London and visited friends at Scotland Yard and elsewhere. On July 6th I went to France with another party of friends, and on July 8th, I called on Ernest Carnot, son of President Carnot, and Maurice de

Jouliatt, my companions in the trip across the Andes Mountains in South America. I met also high officials in the French detective service, and I am frank to say that, of all the detective systems in the world with which I am familiar, I believe the system in vogue in Paris to be the most efficient, the ablest in conception, and the most effective in execution. I speak not of the public idea of what this system is, but of the secret workings of it, the years of training, the culling of men from all walks of life for the detective service, and the consequent ability to reach any line of life, any stratum of society, through agents familiar with all its phases. I had a royal good time in Paris. Paris is an inspiration to mellow memories. It is the capital of the world. I left it on July 10th, amid many adieus, and returned to London, where I spent several days, and on July 14th went to Liverpool, where I had a pleasant visit with Chief Inspector McConkey. He and I laughed over Parisian ways and I found that I had received a thorough introduction to life as it is lived in the city of splendid pleasures.

"I went to Ireland on July 15th. I spent several days in Dublin, and thence went to Sligo, where I had an enjoyable time and owed much of my pleasure to the brother of Lord Dunraven, of yachting fame on this side of the Atlantic. From Sligo I went to Derry, and after further jaunts in Ireland I sailed on July 24th, on the steamer *Vancouver*, for Montreal. I arrived in Quebec on August 1st, 1896, in Montreal on August 2nd, and in Toronto on August 3rd.

"The world is full of surprises. I was walking in Paris when I came face to face with one of my acquaintances in the Buenos Ayres colony of fugitives. He greeted me effusively, and said he was on his way to Russia. He gave me the latest news of the hunted ones in South America, and all the gossip of the tropics of interest to pursuers and pursued. He had his own establishment in Paris and looked like a fashionable clubman. In response to his cordial invitation to visit him I extended an equally cordial invitation to him to stay out of Canada. He thanked me heartily and said he never had been there and never expected to be. He inquired about several crooks.

"'Registered at the Hotel Kingston,' was his phrase for their abiding place.

"I was with a French detective official at the time I met this laugher-at-law and, as we walked on, the official, in casual conversation, went over the entire career of this man and remarked that he was expected to leave Paris the next day. He left.

"I had an opportunity in Paris to observe the careful training given to detectives there. They are taken as young men and from various walks of life, from good families, and are placed with older, experienced men, and for months they go about, learning the faces and ways and lives of crooks of all kinds, lofty and low, convicted and unconvicted. They are educated, drilled, schooled for their work. They serve an apprenticeship as for a trade, they study as for a profession. This is as it should be. The failures are weeded out, the fittest survive. As the world grows and the throngs of humanity increase, the detection of crime will demand trained detectives, equipped for their career as men are equipped for other occupations and professions. Educated men, of trained intellect, will be needed as well as men whose instinctive bent is for the detective business regardless of any general knowledge of life at large. France is on the right road in this respect. I saw the Parisian detectives at work. They are clever men. They know their city like the alphabet. What a city it is! Trivialities and tragedies, with even the tragedies ofttimes ignored as trivial."

33

OLIVE ADELE SEVENPIPER STERNAMAN

OLIVE ADELE SEVENPIPER was tall for her years, even as a child. Her childhood was spent in the township of Rainham, county of Haldimand, her family living near the Sternaman family.

"I was born in Canada," she said, in telling in 1896 the story of her life, "near the home of the Sternamans not far from Rainham Centre. I moved to Buffalo, New York, with my parents when twelve years old. That was in 1879, as I was born in 1867 and am now twenty-nine years old. A few years after settling in Buffalo I went to do general housework for a Mr. Simpson on Lafayette Avenue. I worked there three years and there I met Ezra E. Chipman, who was a carpenter and had come from Canada. He courted me while I worked for Mr. Simpson, and February 3rd, 1886, we were married, and went to live on Hampshire Street, in Buffalo. Two children were born, one in 1887 and one in 1889. Both are living."

Chipman was a prudent man. His life was insured, he took home his earnings, and all went well. George H. Sternaman, a son of the Sternamans who lived near the childhood home of Olive Adele Sevenpiper Chipman, had grown up in Rainham while Miss Sevenpiper was growing up in Buffalo. He became a carpenter, and in 1892 he went to Buffalo to work, being able to obtain better wages there than in the county of Haldimand.

"Sternaman secured board at the home of Olive Adele Sevenpiper Chipman," says Murray. "He and Ezra became fast friends. Both were carpenters and at times they worked together. On January 20th, 1895, Ezra died. George mourned for his friend and continued to board with the widow. On February 3rd, 1896, a little over a year after Ezra died,

186

George married the widow, who became Olive Adele Seven-piper Chipman Sternaman. On August 14th, 1896, George died. He had suffered, and finally had insisted on being taken home to his mother in the township of Rainham, and there he died. The mother, turning from her dead son to the widow, said that it was peculiar her two husbands should die within two years and from the same cause—paralysis.

"'Why, mother, do you mean to insinuate that I had anything to do with their deaths?' said the widow.

"'Yes,' retorted the mother. 'I blame you for poisoning them, blame you until you prove yourself innocent.'

"The mother's tongue started the talk. It spread. In due time the matter was brought to the attention of the Department, and in October 1896 I went to Cayuga to make inquiries concerning Sternaman's death. I had the body exhumed and the viscera sent to Professor Ellis, in Toronto. He found arsenical poisoning. I went to Buffalo and saw Dr. Rich and Dr. Parmenter, who had attended Ezra Chipman. Dr. Rich later testified that in Chipman's last illness his symptoms were gastric vomiting, intense thirst, and later numbness and paralysis, and it might have been caused by arsenic or any other irritant poison. Dr. Parmenter, who also attended Chipman in his last illness, found him suffering from paralysis, and thought his death might possibly have been caused by poison. William Martin, of the Buffalo Carpenters' Union, and William Trandall, of Buffalo, told me and later testified as to Chipman eating his lunch, which was supposed to have contained poison. Chipman, soon after eating, complained of a burning sensation in the stomach, and ceased work and went home, never to return to work. I found Martin and Trandall in my search for men who had worked with Chipman and Sternaman.

"I called on Dr. Frost, Dr. Phelps, and Dr. Saltsman in Buffalo, who had attended Sternaman in his illness. Dr. Frost later testified that in July he suspected arsenical poisoning. The doctor had informed the deceased in the presence of Mrs. Sternaman that there were suspicious symptoms of arsenical poisoning and proposed to have him

187

taken to a hospital. He finally agreed to go, but Mrs. Sternaman objected strongly.

"'I mentioned to her,' testified Dr. Frost later, 'that she had one husband die under suspicious circumstances, and asked her how she would like to have another die under suspicious circumstances. It would be better for her own protection that he should go, and she replied : "Doctor, if he dies I will have an autopsy and that will clear me." The patient grew worse.'

"Dr. Frost called in Dr. Phelps, who told him to look for arsenic.

"'On being told that the patient would get better if he got no more arsenic, she replied that he would get no more,' said Dr. Frost.

"Dr. Frost then was dismissed from treating the patient and Dr. Saltsman was called in. Dr. Phelps corroborated Dr. Frost and said he had administered arsenic to patients and that Sternaman's case was identical, only much worse. After Dr. Frost was dismissed Sternaman wanted to go home to Canada. His mother went over to see him and finally he was taken home to Rainham in August. Dr. Clark, of Rainham, attended him at his mother's home and he gave it as his opinion that death was due to poison. Dr. Park, of Selkirk, also attended him before his death in Rainham. He found the patient partially paralysed and totally helpless. The day before he died he vomited.

"'He was suffering from multiple neuritis, brought on from arsenical poisoning,' testified Dr. Park.

"Dr. Harrison, of Selkirk, who saw Sternaman with Dr. Park, testified : 'I am sure he was poisoned by arsenic.'

"I learned that Sternaman's life was insured for $200 in the Carpenters' Union, for $770 in the Hancock Mutual Insurance Company, and for $1,000 in the Metropolitan, this last policy being dated a few months before he died. J. E. Dewey, of Buffalo, a Hancock insurance agent, told me and testified later that he met the widow on Dearborn Street, in Buffalo, and asked her about her husband's death. She asked him not to say anything about the policy on Sternaman's life, as her relatives would get it from her if they knew of it. She received the $770 from the Hancock Company.

"I learned also that the widow had a letter or statement to whom it might concern, signed by her husband and dated June 10th, 1896, over two months before he died, in which he said he hoped that the statement would 'convince all that they may not think that my wife had anything to do with such an uncommon death.'

"Mrs. Sternaman had left Canada and returned to Buffalo. I had her arrested and remanded in October 1896, and prepared extradition papers. She was arraigned before Commissioner Fairchild, in Buffalo. Thayer and Duckwitz appeared for her. She fought extradition. I had the evidence in shape, including the testimony of the undertaker who conducted the preparation of Sternaman's body for burial, John Snyder, of Rainham. Undertaker Snyder made a written statement, in which he positively swore that he did not embalm the body. From the outset the defence fell back on a claim that the body had been embalmed, and that the embalming fluid was responsible for the result of the analysis, of the viscera. This was the bone of contention throughout the entire case. The woman's counsel carried the case to Judge Coxe, of the United States Court, and then to New York on appeal, but they failed in their fight to prevent her extradition. In summing up the case for her, Attorney Thayer concluded with the assertion that: 'They not only have failed to prove the defendant's connection with Sternaman's death, but have failed to prove that it was caused by arsenical poisoning, owing to the shattered testimony of Undertaker Snyder, who does not know whether he embalmed the body or not.' Commissioner Fairchild deemed the evidence sufficient to sustain the charges and Judge Coxe upheld him and was himself upheld on appeal, and after a long fight, in August 1897, a year after Sternaman's death, I took Mrs. Sternaman to Canada and handed her over to the Cayuga authorities, where she was placed in gaol. She was arraigned before a magistrate and committed in September. The grand jury indicted her for murder, and in November 1897 her trial occurred at Cayuga. Chief Justice

Armour presided. B. B. Osler prosecuted, and W. M. German defended, assisted by Wallace Thayer, of Buffalo.

"The evidence, as I have indicated it, was presented. There was a big legal battle. The fact that a woman was on trial for her life gave the trial wide interest and caused excitement as to the outcome. The defence swore a number of witnesses to the effect that, in their opinion, death was not due to arsenic. The Crown's case, however, convinced the jury, and on November 19th Mrs. Olive Adele Sevenpiper Sternaman was found guilty of murder, and was sentenced to be hanged on Thursday, January 20th, 1898.

"'And may God have mercy on your soul,' said Chief Justice Armour.

"'Oh, Judge! Is there no mercy in this country?' gasped the woman, grey-faced, black-gowned, dry-eyed.

"She was led out to her cell.

"Her counsel applied for a reserve case on the ground of the irrelevancy of the Chipman evidence. The woman's friends rallied to her support. Many people were opposed to the hanging of a woman. The Rev. J. D. Edgar and other ministers befriended her. The case was carried to Ottawa. An affidavit of Dr. Thompson, that embalming fluid was found in the body, was presented, with petitions, to the authorities at Ottawa. Strenuous efforts were made to obtain a second trial.

"Meanwhile the scaffold was a-building in the gaolyard at Cayuga. The sound of the hammers could be heard by the woman in her cell. She made ready to die. The last week began. No word came from Ottawa. Monday passed; Thursday she was to die. Her friends and their sympathisers rallied for a final effort. Tuesday came and went. Late on Tuesday night a telegram from Ottawa announced that after a long discussion by the Dominion Cabinet it had been decided to grant a new trial.

"The second trial occurred in the spring of 1898, before Chancellor Boyd of Cayuga. B. B. Osler prosecuted. At this trial the undertaker swore he had embalming fluid and needle with him when he prepared the body. It was a long trial. The jury found a verdict of not guilty. Mrs. Olive Adele Sevenpiper Chipman Sternaman went free."

34

FOOLISH FRANK OSIER AND WISE SAM LINDSAY

FRANK OSIER at one time lived in Rodney, in the county of Elgin. He courted Martha McCartney, the buxom daughter of William McCartney, a tailor. The tailor frowned on his suit, but the daughter beamed on Osier and ignored her father's warning. Osier pressed his suit in the hope of winning the tailor's approval, but McCartney shook his head. The upshot of the affair was the marriage of Osier and Martha McCartney.

"He has too many trades," said William McCartney to his daughter. "He is a travelling barber, a sewing machine repairer, a clock maker, and several other things. If he does all these by day, how do you know that he may not have a lot more trades that he practises by night—burglary, for instance?"

The daughter tossed her pretty head, and was married just the same. A few years later she was dead.

"Her death occurred on August 2nd, 1897," says Murray. "Her father, William McCartney, the tailor, immediately suspected foul play, and he demanded an inquest and communicated with the Department in an urgent request for an investigation. I went to Rodney. Dr. Van Buskirk made a post-mortem examination and stated that, to the best of his knowledge, death was caused solely by an operation, performed under circumstances unknown, and the coroner's jury found a verdict accordingly. Mr. McCartney insisted that Osier had killed his wife.

"Osier had disappeared from Rodney after his wife's death. There had been several burglaries before his departure. The stores of Mistele Brothers and of Martins Brothers and others had been robbed. William McCartney, on the morning after the Mistele burglary, had visited the store and said Osier had a hand in the deed, and asserted that his unwelcome son-in-law was in league with a gang of burglars, and travelled from place to place, sojourning in each town long enough to get acquainted and lay the plans to burglarise the richest people or stores in the vicinity. There was no evidence at the time, and the matter drifted along until the tailor's daughter died and Osier went away. He skipped for the United States and crossed to Marine City, where United States Customs' officers spotted him, and suspected him of smuggling and arrested him. He gave a fictitious name and was sent to gaol, as a quantity of cloth and other stolen stuff was recovered when he was taken. A search of his clothes brought to light an undertaker's receipt for funeral preliminaries for Martha McCartney Osier. This receipt revealed Osier's real name, and I was informed of his arrest. I went to Detroit and had Canada owners identify their stolen property. I began extradition proceedings, and on July 25th, 1898, Osier was turned over to me

" ' I'd prefer to walk to the station, if it's all the same to you, Mr. Murray,' said Osier.

" ' Certainly,' said I, and we started.

" He had smiled when I agreed to walk and it put me on my guard. We were walking below the Russell House, when Osier made a break for liberty. He sidled off toward the curb and suddenly darted across the street. He had been shifting and side-stepping for five minutes before he dashed away, so I was forewarned, and, as he started, I put out my foot. He tripped and fell headlong, but jumped up and started again. I grabbed him, he struck at me, and down we went and had it out. A policeman came along and shoved the crowd back, and the policeman and I picked Osier up and carried him to the curb. When he opened his eyes he kicked out again. We had it out right there on the side-walk in Detroit for the second time. The policeman called the patrol waggon.

" ' I'll never go to Canada alive ! ' shouted Osier.

" ' You certainly won't if you keep this up much longer,' I informed him.

" Osier looked at me.

" ' Well, I'll do my best,' he said, and he did. So did I.

"When it was over we picked Osier up and laid him in the patrol waggon and drove to the station and carried him on to the train, and when he really roused himself we were in Canada and nearing St. Thomas. He said he felt considerably shaken up, and he looked it. He was tried in September, and on Wednesday, September 21st, 1898, was convicted and sent to Kingston Penitentiary for four and a-half years for burglary.

"During the past few years they have been trying the ticket-of-leave business to some extent at Kingston. Osier thus got out before his time expired, his liberty being dependent on his good behaviour. He married another wife. It was the intention of the Crown to have Osier answer McCartney's charge of killing his daughter, but owing to the diversity of opinion among the medical men who made the post-mortem it was considered difficult, if not futile, to undertake to obtain a conviction on the evidence available at that time.

"About this same time I had Sam Lindsay on my hands, too. Sam was an expert bank-breaker. He had a criminal record extending over a score of years. He had been convicted of burglary at Simcoe, and served a term in the common gaol, from which he promptly escaped. He was captured and served a term in Kingston. He bobbed up in 1882, and burglarised Flamboro Post Office, and again was sentenced to Kingston. On the way to the Penitentiary he broke away from Sheriff Gibson and disappeared. A few months later he was caught in a burglary near Windsor, Vermont, and was sentenced to fourteen years in the Vermont penitentiary under the name of R. R. Ferguson. Between the time of his escape from Sheriff Gibson and his arrest in Vermont he had quarrelled with a man in a resort on St. Justin Street, Montreal, and had shot the man in the neck. He was arrested then under the name of Knox, and was held, but the wounded man recovered and disappeared, and Sam got away. After he was released in Vermont he turned up again in Montreal, and was recognised and taken for the escape from Sheriff Gibson. Sam was suspected also of being concerned in two robberies shortly before his arrest in Montreal. One was the Anderson's Bank robbery in Oakville, and the other was the Hunt's Bank robbery in Bracebridge. Sam was slippery and he had a good alibi for these two charges. So I took him to Hamilton to stand trial on the charge of escaping from custody in 1882.

"Sam immediately began to talk mysteriously of buried treasure. It did not work. I reminded him that when he was in Kingston years before he had professed sudden piety, and in evidence of his reformation had told the warden that he knew a place near Hagersville, where a great quantity of counterfeit plates, genuine bonds, and other stolen property had been buried, and he had promised to reveal the place if taken there. I had no faith in this story, but Sam was taken to the spot of which he told. He looked around and finally said that the mark had been removed and he could not locate the booty. About that time I had given Sam my opinion of such monkey-business. Sam coolly answered :

"'I was taking my chance for liberty. How could I tell who would come with me?'

"I refreshed Sam's memory in Hamilton of this episode years before, and told him it would not work a second time.

"'If you were in my place, Murray, you would forget that first time,' said Sam.

"Sam made a legal fight, and the Minister of Justice decided that Sam had to be apprehended within three years after the date of his escape, so he went free.

"Sam smiled. He had a sense of humour, and some of his burglaries he regarded as jokes. When he escaped the joke was on the other fellow ; when he was caught the joke was on him. Whichever way it went Sam smiled."

35

EDDIE ELLIOTT, BOY MURDERER

A FEW years after Eddie Elliott was big enough to walk, many of the cats on the outskirts of Beaverton, in the county of Ontario, became sightless. They groped about with empty sockets, from which the eyeballs appeared to have been plucked. Many of the dogs lost their tails and their ears. At night three or four dogs would rush yelping across the country, terrified by tin cans or agonised by turpentine. Eddie meanwhile went fishing, with cats' eyeballs for bait, and collected tin cans and stole turpentine and continued his torture of beasts and all animate things on which he dared lay his hands. He grew to be fifteen, and if he had lived a few centuries earlier he probably would have gone gallivant-ing forth as a red knight with a dripping sword above an eyeless head for his coat of arms.

"As it was, he went to work for old William Murray, a retired farmer, who had turned four score years," says Murray. "Eddie did chores for old William, who lived alone in a little house of a single room, twenty by sixteen feet, standing back from the Beaverton Road. He had the lad come occasionally and do odd bits of work about the place. William's bosom friend was John McHattie, another old chap, who would sit the day through with his crony while they talked of what occurred fifty years and more ago. John McHattie could recite the descriptions of many farms in the counties round-about, and relate in detail the course of their titles from the day an axe first felled a tree upon them. Old William was full of the events of threescore years ago. He would sit in a big chair and rock to and fro while John McHattie told again of the clearing of some one's farm two generations earlier.

"On Tuesday, November 15th, 1898, old William was

found dead in his house. The Department was notified and I went to the place immediately. The old man had been found lying in a pool of blood. Near by lay an iron poker, with blood and hair on it, and in poking about we found a cordwood stick, about four feet long, with traces of the tragedy staining it. Old John McHattie was grieving for his dead crony. McHattie and I sat down together, and he told me that the last time he saw William alive was on the preceding Saturday. McHattie had called about half-past three in the afternoon. Eddie Elliott was there at the time. William gave $1 to McHattie to get some provisions. McHattie went away and got them and returned, giving to William seventy cents change, as the provisions had cost thirty cents. McHattie saw William take out his pocket-book, put the seventy cents in it, and put it in his pocket.

" 'We talked of old times when the world was not getting so crowded and then I went away,' said McHattie. 'I left William sitting in his chair with Eddie Elliott sitting near by.'

" 'What was Elliott doing?'

" 'Nothing—just sitting there, idly swinging a poker,' said McHattie.

" McHattie said that the next day, Sunday, he called, as was his custom, but found the house locked. This was unusual, as he and William usually talked on Sundays of sermons of years before and of big crops.

" 'Crops and sermons, sermons and crops, were our Sunday talking, and they made most congenial conversation,' said old John McHattie.

" Sorely disappointed to find the house locked, McHattie went home and moped all day Sunday, and bright and early on Monday went again to see his friend William. The house still was locked, and no one answered the knock. On Tuesday McHattie went again to see William. He knew William had not gone on a jaunt, for he was lame and feeble, and spent his days chiefly in his chair. For William to go on a journey without telling McHattie and discussing it solemnly with him, would have been as unlikely as for McHattie to go to heaven without dying—something that has not occurred since the days of the prophets. McHattie, with other neighbours,

196

thumped on William's door, and watched the chimney for sign of smoke, and listened at the door and window for sound of William. Then, seeing no smoke, hearing no sound, the door was broken in, and William was found dead, with his head beaten in.

"I looked for the pocket-book; it was gone. I looked for tracks; there were none. I searched for a place where the murderer washed his hands; I found none. I hunted for the key to the door; it could not be found. Common sense pointed the finger of suspicion at Eddie Elliott. I made full inquiries concerning him, and learnt of his plucking the eyes out of cats and using them for fish-bait, and of his torturing dumb animals, of his abusing horses, of his seeming delight in cruelties and brutalities. The crime, of course, had aroused the people. Many believed it impossible for a fifteen-year-old boy to have done the deed, and they scouted the idea that Eddie Elliott was the murderer. They asserted that a robber had done the murder, sneaking in upon the old man at night and escaping, with many miles between him and his victim, before the crime was discovered. I talked with the neighbours and with others, hearing what they had to offer, and all the while mindful of Eddie Elliott. I learned from little Beatrice Gardner, living near by, that she had seen Elliott leave Murray's house on Saturday afternoon, some time after John McHattie had gone. The boy was her chum. She saw blood on his hand when he stopped to chat with her.

" ' What's the matter ? ' she asked.

" ' I fell on the ice and cut it,' said Eddie Elliott.

" David McFee later saw Elliott with the old man's pocket-book. McFee knew old William and young Eddie well. Shortly before old William was killed, Eddie Elliott had stolen a horse from Reeve McMillan, of Beaverton. He was overtaken before he sold it, and his explanation was he simply had borrowed it.

" I went to see Eddie Elliott. I walked in and stopped short, for I seemed to see Jim Allison, the seventeen-year-old murderer of Mrs. Orr, near Galt. Jim Allison had been hanged, yet here stood Jim Allison or his double.

" ' What is your name ? ' I asked.

" ' Eddie Elliott,' he answered.

197

" The voice was Jim Allison's voice. The head was Jim Allison's head, with the low brow and the frog-like face. The eyes were Jim Allison's eyes ; the hair was Jim Allison's hair. I had not thought there was another boy in the province like Allison, yet here stood simpering Jim Allison's duplicate, so like him as to seem as if Jim had arisen from the dead. Mentally he was Allison's duplicate, as well as physically. He was strong, like Jim.

" ' How old are you ? ' I asked.

" ' A couple of months short of sixteen,' he answered.

" I looked at him, feeling as if I were talking to Jim Allison again.

" ' You have blood on your hands,' I said abruptly.

" He paled. He was guilty as if the whole world had seen him club the old man to death, as William sat in his chair, and then steal the seventy cents and whatever else was valuable.

" Constable Smith took him to find the missing key of William's door. The boy had hid a key under the sidewalk ; it was the wrong key. The right key was found at the boy's home. We took the youth to Whitby gaol to await trial. His father called to see him.

" ' Eddie, did you kill poor old Murray ? ' asked his father.

" ' Yes I did,' said Eddie bluntly.

" ' Who was with you ? '

" ' I was all alone ; I did not want anybody with me,' said this murderer, who was not sixteen years old.

" The father made a deposition setting forth that his son had confessed himself a murderer. He cried bitterly as he signed the affidavit.

" Eddie Elliott was tried at Whitby, and was convicted of murder on May 23rd, 1899. Justice McMahon presided, and the boy was sentenced to be hanged on August 17th. He took it philosophically. His parents strove to save his life ; he was only fifteen, they pleaded. Others assisted them in their efforts. Instead of being hanged and buried in an unmarked grave in a prison-yard, like Jim Allison, this boy murderer, Eddie Elliott, was buried alive. His sentence was commuted to imprisonment for life. If he lives to the age of his victim, he will serve sixty-four years inside four grey walls."

36

DEMURE KATE PENDER OF EMSDALE

MANY a country town in Canada boasts, among the other triumphs of its civilisation, an elaborate millinery store. The village of Emsdale, near Parry Sound, was no exception. The village milliner was Kate Pender, demure, yet vivacious. Her life was spotless, blameless, flawless, so far as the villagers knew. She went to church, lived quietly, had a kindly word and a cheery smile for old and young, and was regarded as one of those for whom already a crown of gold was set aside in the radiant hereafter. She would have made a charming angel, with her pink cheeks and sunny smile and sparkling eyes. The sunlight on her hair made it golden, and there were those who said celestial music murmured in her voice. Like other country milliners, she made occasional trips to the centres of fashion, there to note the latest styles in hats, and later improve upon the novelties she had seen. Thus from Paris to Emsdale travelled the triumphant bewilderments of bonnets, the route being by way of Toronto and other intermediate points.

" But we often cannot judge by appearances," says Murray. " To all appearances Kate Pender was a model of all the angelic virtues. Oliver Campbell Fish would have averred it on a stack of Bibles as high as the pyramids of Egypt. Fish managed a general store at Emsdale for his brother, R. Y. Fish. He and Kate Pender became acquaintances, then friends, and finally they disappeared.

" R. Y. Fish complained to the Department that his brother had appropriated goods to the amount of $6,000, together with sums of money taken at various times and unaccounted for. He accused the fair Kate Pender of taking quantities of dress goods from his establishment. He said he had searched for the missing pair in vain. I set out to find them. I went to Emsdale, and looked over the remaining effects of Oliver Campbell Fish and Kate Pender. I found nothing that would give any clue in Fish's effects. Among the articles left behind by Kate Pender was a bustle. From what I could learn in the village, Kate Pender had no occasion to wear a bustle, and, in fact, bustles had been out of style for some time, and Kate Pender was not given to wearing things that were out of fashion. I came to the conclusion, therefore, that the bustle did not necessarily belong to the fair Kate Pender.

"I picked it up curiously and turned it over, and, to my surprise, a railway map fluttered to the floor. I dropped the bustle and picked up the folder. I glanced at it casually, and was about to toss it aside, when I noticed a pencil line drawn on the railroad map in the State of Iowa. I examined it minutely then, and on a list of trains I found a similar pencil mark drawn. The mark on the map stopped at Ackley, Iowa. The scratch on the list of trains stopped at Dubuque, Iowa. Ackley was not far from Dubuque. I took this for a possible clue, and looked up, on the railroads, any possible trace of the baggage of the missing pair. This line of research was not particularly fruitful, so I decided to go to Ackley and look around for the vanished couple. I arrived in Ackley in April 1899. The fair Kate Pender was out for a promenade, and I saw her on the street.

"Back to Dubuque I went, executed the necessary papers, and returned to Ackley. There I met the fair Kate Pender and Oliver Campbell Fish, and invited them to attend a legal function at Parry Sound as the guests of the Government. They thought it over and accepted, waiving the forms of extradition. I brought them back on April 29th, 1899, and took them to Parry Sound to await the action of the authorities there on this case.

"R. Y. Fish, who had complained to the Department that his brother had stolen practically enough to stock a store, seemed to relent after a talk with his brother and the fair Kate Pender. I understood the matter was settled by the brothers, and after the settlement Oliver Campbell Fish went away, taking Kate Pender with him.

"I burned the bustle. After I saw the fair Kate Pender I knew she had no use for it, and, moreover, it probably never had been worn by her at all. Yet, as I remarked at the outset of this case, we cannot always judge by appearances.

"It was the only case in my career in which I found a clue in a bustle."

37

LEE CLUEY OF CATHAY

LEE CLUEY was a Chinese laundryman. He had a little
shop in the village of Norwich, in the county of Oxford.
His eyes were like beads set in almonds, and his skin was
the colour of a brass kettle. He kept a big black cat, with
a little silver bell tied round its neck with yellow ribbon.
For a time he also had a green poll-parrot, with a yellow head.
He loved yellow, did Lee Cluey. His long pipe of seven
puffs had yellow bands round it. He wore a yellow stone
in a yellow ring. On his left arm he wore a big yellow
bracelet. In fact, if ever there was a yellow fellow it was this
amber-handed, saffron-faced son of Cathay.

"His face was like the front of a yellow house," says
Murray. "When you looked at him down went the blinds—
he closed his eyes lest you should see inside. He had pros-
pered in his little shop in Norwich, where he had been living
for three years. He was fond of working by the open door
and passers-by could hear the thump of his iron as he sang in
a high falsetto, his finest arias being a series of jerky squeaks,
as if a rat with a very bad cold were shouting for the police
to rescue it from the clutches of Trap, the strangler. The
poll-parrot was a finicky creature, for it would ruffle up when
Lee Cluey sang.

"'Chokee off, Cluey! Chokee off!' it would squawk.

"Few people knew that Lee Cluey had this parrot, as he
kept it in a back room, and, truth to tell, its squawkings were
much like Cluey's singing, particularly the high notes. The
parrot, however, came to know some of Cluey's customers
by sight, as it peered out of the gloom of the back room, and
it muttered comments on callers incessantly.

"Cluey was quick to learn that his best customers were
among the churchpeople. So Cluey went to church. He
would sally forth out of his little shop with clasped hands
and waddle solemnly to worship, sitting stoically from

201

beginning to end of the service. Then back to his shop he toddled, his duty done. In 1899 a series of small thefts annoyed residents of the village. Lee Cluey heard the talk, but sang on during week days and went to church on Sundays. Some hinted that Cluey might know something of the thefts, but others indignantly denied it, and said they had seen Cluey at church regularly for many Sundays. One Sunday in November Lee Cluey went to church as usual and trotted home briskly. He entered his shop, poked up the fire, took his pipe of seven puffs and was about to settle down in comfort, when he sprang up with a long, loud squawk. He rushed out into the November night and trotted through the streets.

"'Thievee! Thievee!' he repeated, over and over.

"Then the mayor sent a complaint to the Department and I went to investigate. Cluey said that while he was at church a back window of his shop had been forced and a small metal trunk, in which his most precious possessions were stored, had been stolen. He mourned particularly the loss of money. He said he had a cigar-box full of it in the trunk.

"I examined the premises and could find no clue to the identity of the thieves. Cluey followed me about and the cat rubbed up against me while the parrot turned away in disgust.

"'Get out, Healy, get out,' it muttered at me, so naturally that I laughed.

"The parrot fluffed up.

"'Getee hellee outee!' it squawked.

"I nosed around the village and found no tangible traces of the thieves and then I walked back to Cluey's shop and looked in the window the thieves had forced.

"'Get out, Healy, get out!' said the parrot vehemently.

"I walked away.

"'Do you know anyone named Healy?' I asked an acquaintance.

"'There's a young fellow named Louis Healy,' he answered.

"'Who are his friends, his favourite associates?'

"'Fred Rawlings and William Poldon,' was the reply.

"I went after Healy. He was not pleased to see me.

"'A witness saw you at Lee Cluey's window,' said I.

"Healy gasped. He and Rawlings and Poldon were questioned separately by me. Under examination they confessed the crime. They produced the cigar box and turned over $45, which they said was all it contained. The metal trunk was recovered. They had hid it on the bank of a creek. Lee Cluey fell on his knees beside it when he saw it.

"'You getee $911?' he asked.

"'No, only $45,' said I.

"Lee Cluey was loud in his lamentations. I questioned Healy, Rawlings, and Poldon again. They vowed that $45 was all the money they had found in the trunk and that they had turned over all that they had stolen. Of course, although a liar is not always a thief, a thief invariably is a liar as well. But the three young fellows stuck earnestly to their story. I went back to Lee Cluey's shop.

"'You getee my fifteen hundred dollees?' asked Lee Cluey.

"I stared at him. Fifteen hundred! His loss had grown since I last saw him. He had declared first it was $911. Back I went to the three prisoners. They stoutly averred that $45 was the total of the money in the trunk. I returned to Cluey's.

"'You getee my two thousand dollees?' said Cluey.

"He never smiled. I suppose he would have raised it to $5,000 if I had made two or three more trips to and fro.

"'Cluey,' I said, 'you have jumped from $900 to $2,000.'

"'Two thousand five hundred dollees,' interrupted Lee Cluey shrilly.

"'Chokee off, Cluey! Chokee off!' squawked the parrot.

"I began to laugh and walked out, leaving Lee Cluey jargoning and lashing his queue at the parrot. The three thieves went to prison."

38

THE THREE DYNAMITARDS

KINGSTON PENITENTIARY, where the desperate criminals and all long-term convicts of the Province are confined, looms a huge mass of grey stone on the shore of the St. Lawrence River. One side of the grim, high walls fronts on the water's edge. When night falls over Kingston and the long lines of convicts have gone to their cells with bolts and locks all fastened and secure, three men sit alone in three widely separate cells. Along the silent corridors go the velvet-slippered guards, their footfalls noiseless in their steady patrol. Occasionally a watchman stops and peers in. All is quiet; the three men seemingly are asleep. When morning comes they are up with the sun and through the dull day they go their dreary way, to the stone pile where the hammers rise and fall, or to the workshop where mutely they toil. Each is known by a number. Their sentence is for life. The great grey prison is the receiving vault to their eternal tomb. They are buried alive.

Life is over for them. The future is a blank existence, bounded by four grim, grey walls. Friends, family, loved ones, home, happiness, all are bygone. Their companions now and through the future years are criminals who shuffle speechlessly, ceaselessly, on their weary road of punishment. The one glimpse of the world comes to them through the window of memory in visions of the vanished years. It is a living death and, saving one ever-cherished hope, the only change that will come will be a closing of the eyes, a stilling of the pulse, and then a creaking of the prison gates to let a hearse go by bearing them to smaller, darker cells.

The ever-cherished hope! When years have softened the hearts of men and mercy moves them to generous forgiveness, it is the convict's endless yearning that a bit of paper may arrive to open his cell and let the punished man go free. It is the hope of pardon shining brightly into desolate lives— and none ever can tell what the far future years may bring forth.

"The crime for which these three men went to Kingston," says Murray, "occurred at Thorold, at seven o'clock on the evening of Saturday, April 21st, 1900. It resounded in two thunderous explosions that tore up solid rocks, tossed sky-ward spouts of water, shook houses and shattered windows, while the earth trembled. For miles around people paused, terrified, amazed, or dumbfounded. They waited, as if for the aftermath, for a descent of death and destruction, for the swoop of a calamity that would wipe them and their homes from the face of the earth. It did not come. But by how small a chance it failed, is something that to this day sends shuddering those who saw the dreadful crime.

"Thorold is a Canadian hamlet. It nestles along the waterway of the Welland Canal, the Dominion's channel of commerce between Lakes Erie and Ontario. It is within easy walking distance of the frontier at Niagara Falls and is in the general vicinity of the border towns from St. Catherine's to Clifton on the Niagara River by the Falls. Lock No. 24 of the Welland Canal is at Thorold. Above it, in the canal, is a level about one mile long, forty feet wide and twenty feet deep, with a second level, No. 25, beyond it. There is a drop of sixteen feet in the lock, and from it on to Lake Ontario, there is a series of drops, each level being lower like a series of steps, down which the waters made their way. The gates of the Thorold lock hold in placid check twelve million cubic feet of water, and the sudden smashing of the gates would have released this miniature sea and transformed it from an unruffled expanse of still water to a rushing, roaring, seething, furious torrent, surging in a deadly deluge over the lock, over the lower levels, obliterating their gate, freeing their floods of waters ; raging over the Grand Trunk Railroad tracks and spreading out in angry, awful flood into the valley of Ten Mile Creek ; wiping out homes and houses, ruining lands, devastating property, and, worst of all, ghastliest of all, drowning hundreds of innocent people and obliterating the town of Merritton. It would have paralysed Canada's great waterway, prostrating her water trade from the great lakes.

"Eyewitnesses saw the explosion. Miss Euphemia Constable, a pretty sixteen-year-old girl, who lived with her parents about three hundred yards from the lock No. 24, was going to see a friend across the canal about 6.20. Near the bridge, which is by the lock, she saw two men. One was going down by the tool-house to the other end of the lock. The other was standing at the end of the bridge and then walked to the swing bridge. He laid down a valise or brown telescope he was carrying and got off the bridge. She passed him within five feet. He had one hand on the valise and the other at his face, but he moved the hand at his face and she saw his face clearly. He stepped through the side of the bridge and off the bridge from the middle, and took the valise to the end of the lock. Thus at each end of the lock stood one of the men and each had a valise. Miss Constable saw the man at the other end of the lock take a rope and tie it to the end of his valise.

"'I walked on,' said Miss Constable later, 'and then I heard the man farthest away cry: "Hurry on, Jack, or it'll go off!" and he ran down the road leading to the Falls. I turned and saw the second man had not tied the rope to his valise yet. He finally tied it on, dropped the valise into the lock, sprang up on to the bridge, and ran after the first man on the road to the Falls.'

"Then came the explosions. After the first explosion the girl lost consciousness and knew nothing of the second explosion. The explosion was of dynamite contained in the valises dangled into the lock. They were not quite simultaneous. They were fired by fuzes. They broke the castings on the head gate, tore up the banks on both sides of the lock, knocked people over who were sufficiently near and smashed windows and shook the country roundabout. Water rose skyward, but the gates held. The dynamiters had blundered by lowering the dynamite into the gate pits instead of into the chain holes. Experts later showed that there was not sufficient resistance to the explosive matter and that this fact alone prevented the dire disaster that would have followed, if the dynamite had done the work planned for it and had smashed the gates.

"After lowering the satchels into the lock, the two men ran and were about twelve hundred feet from the lock when the first explosion occurred and the other immediately followed. They reached the Stone Road, or public highway, leading to Niagara Falls and hurried along it toward the border. The Mayor of Thorold and others, after the first terror and excitement had passed, followed in buggies along the Stone Road, other citizens taking other roads. The Mayor of Thorold passed the two men on the Stone Road, and arrived at the Falls ahead of them. The two men arrived at the Falls on the Canada side about 8.45 p.m., and were pointed out by the Thorold people and were arrested. A third man, who had been seen around with them before the explosion, and who was at the Rosli House at the Falls, also was arrested. The two men gave their names as John Nolin and John Walsh. The third man gave his name as Karl Dallman. The three men were locked up. Intense excitement followed. Wild rumours were spread abroad. The soldiery were called out. The three prisoners were taken to Welland gaol and guarded by soldiers, while other soldiers patrolled the canal. There were tales of midnight prowlers, of shots in the dark, of mysterious phantoms. There were various theories as to the crime. The excitement along the border grew.

"I found Dallman a stout, grey-haired, full-faced, smooth-shaven man of about fifty. Nolin was short and brown moustached, and looked a prosperous mechanic. Walsh was tall, red faced, smooth shaven and watery eyed. I had them photographed in Welland gaol. Dallman smashed the camera and made a break for liberty. I pulled my revolver and we had quite a tussle. Dallman strove to dash through the door. I halted him and forced him back and then locked him in a cell. He was a desperate man. Nolin and Walsh stood together as if Dallman were a stranger to them. Dallman said he was fifty years old, born in England, a clerk, married, a Methodist, and Buffalo the last place of residence.

He said he knew nothing of any dynamite explosion or any plot to do harm.

"'I went on a spree,' he said. 'I did no harm. I knew nothing of any plot to do harm, and I never knew Walsh or Nolin until I met them while on a spree at Niagara Falls.'

"The evidence at the magistrate's hearing and at the trial was voluminous. Charles Lindenfield, of the Stafford House, in Buffalo, told of Dallman arriving there in March, going away, returning again on March 22nd, and again on April 11th, and again on April 14th, registering as Karl Dallman, of Trenton, New Jersey. On April 15th he was joined at the Stafford House, in Buffalo, by Nolin and Walsh, under the names of Smith and Moore. Lindenfield told of their meeting. Sergeant Maloney, of the Niagara Falls, New York Police, told of seeing Dallman, Nolin, and Walsh together in a trolley car at the Falls at ten o'clock on Thursday night, April 19th. Charles E. Lewis, a United States Secret Service man at the Falls, noticed the men together by reason of their frequent crossing of the cantilever bridge to Canada. He tracked Nolin, Walsh, and Dallman together to a room in the Dolphin House the day before the explosion. On the day of the explosion he saw Dallman and Nolin together with a package. On the night of the explosion he searched the room in the Dolphin House, and found two coils of fuse and a dynamite rubber pouch. Customs Officer W. F. Latta saw Nolin and Dallman with a package the day before the explosion, and saw Walsh carry the satchels across the bridge into Canada, one on Friday with Nolin, and one on Saturday. Joe Spencer, a cabman, identified Dallman, Nolin, and Walsh, as three men who hired him to drive them from the upper to the lower steel arch bridge a day or two before the explosion, Dallman paying for the cab. On Thursday, two days before the explosion, Spencer drove Nolin and Walsh to Thorold, where they took a walk. While returning to Thorold they passed Dallman driving on the road leading past lock No. 24. Owen Riley, of St. Catharine's, on a train from Merriton to Thorold, saw and talked with Dallman two days before the explosion. Dallman got off at Thorold, and Riley showed him where to hire a buggy,

George Thomas, a clerk in Taylor's store at the Falls, told of selling to Walsh, while Nolin waited outside, the rope used to lower the satchels into the lock. The rope was bought about 8 p.m. on the day of the explosion. George Walters corroborated George Thomas. Miss Alma Cleveland of Thorold, saw Walsh and Nolin get off the train at Thorold with the satchels and the parcel containing the rope on the evening of the explosion. Mrs. Slingerland, of Catharine Street, Thorold, saw them as they walked from the train. William Chapel saw them pass his house within sight of the lock. Miss Euphemia Constable told of seeing them lower the satchels into the lock. Her mother told of seeing Dallman, Nolin, and Walsh at the lock on the Monday before the explosion. They were looking it over. Dan Parr, a watchman at the lock, heard a splash, and saw the men leaving, and then was knocked down by the explosion. Miss Mary Gregory and Mrs. Rebecca Gregory, her mother, passed the men on the Falls road after the explosion. William Pierce, a working man, fell in with them on the road to the Falls, and walked as far as Stamford, they saying nothing of the explosion. George Black saw them on the road, and followed them in his buggy. The Mayor of Thorold told of following and passing them. Alfred Burrows, of the Rosli House, told of Karl Dallman registering at his hotel from Washington, D.C., on April 12th and on April 16th, and of John Walsh, of Washington, D.C., being there on April 19th. Dr. Houseberger told of dressing three burns on Walsh's hand after his arrest. Officer Mains told of the actions of Dallman, Nolin, and Walsh together at the Falls on days before the explosion, and of their arrest after the explosion. Fred Latta, on the day before the explosion, walked up the street at the Falls behind Dallman and Walsh for two blocks. He was about four feet behind them. He heard Dallman say to Walsh :

" ' Do you know where Jack is ? '

" ' I suppose he is getting drunk,' replied Walsh.

" ' If we don't keep that —— sober we will never be able to pull off that job,' was Dallman's answer.

" ' How are we going to keep him sober ? ' said Walsh.

" ' If we can't do it any other way we will have to lock him in a room.'

" They passed on, and later met Nolin, who was carrying a parcel, which he handed to Dallman, and later took it back. All the witnesses identified the men positively. The Crown showed by Edward Walker, an expert on dynamite, that the failure of the explosion to accomplish its object probably was due to lack of sufficient resistance against the explosive. Two engineers testified as to the death and destruction that would have followed the deluge of 12,000,000 feet of water if the explosion had resulted as planned.

" Dallman made a defence ; Nolin and Walsh made none. Dallman tried to prove an alibi by Charles Kinney, a cab-man, attempting to show he had not been at the lock with Nolin and Walsh a few days before the explosion. His alibi was a failure as Kinney became tangled up, and finally Chancellor Boyd remarked that he had made a mess of his evidence. None of the three prisoners went on the stand.

" Their trial began before Chancellor Boyd at Welland on May 25th, 1900. The jury filed out as the clock struck six on the evening of May 26th. They filed in at 6.4. They were out just four minutes.

" ' Guilty,' said the foreman.

" ' All three ? ' asked Chancellor Boyd.

" ' Yes,' said the foreman ; ' all three.'

" The three prisoners arose and faced the court. They had been found guilty, after a fair and careful investigation, of a crime against the State and Crown, said Chancellor Boyd. It was a novel experiment in Canada, he continued, to use explosives to damage a public work. The motive had not been disclosed, and was unknown. In the case of Nolin and Walsh, said the court, it probably was one of hire and for gain. As to Dallman, said his lordship, he was the master spirit, more guilty than the others, and the motive was of hate and a blow against the State and civilisation. It was committed with illegal intent ; it had been long and deliberately planned.

" ' I see no reason for altering the penalty of the indictment, and I sentence all three to imprisonment for life,' concluded the court.

" The three prisoners were put into irons, and marched out and taken to Kingston Penitentiary.

" When it came to ascertaining the details of the past life of the three men, I found a task involving much labour. I communicated with Scotland Yard, and sent them descriptions and photographs ; for Nolin and Walsh seemed unmistakably to be from across the sea, and Walsh particularly had the manner and speech of a man recently over. I went to New York and saw friends there, both in and out of the police business. I went also to Philadelphia, Washington, Virginia, and elsewhere.

" I learned that in Dublin, Ireland, in 1894 were three young men who set sail for America. They were John Nolin, a young machinist; John Rowan, a mechanic ; and John Merna, a mechanic. They arrived in New York, and drifted about the metropolis until, on May 17th, 1894, Merna declared his intention to become a citizen of the United States, took out his first papers, and gave his residence as No. 41, Peck Slip, New York. Nolin went to Philadelphia, and obtained employment in the Baldwin Locomotive Works. In 1895 all three—Nolin, Merna, and Rowan—returned to Ireland. Merna got a job on the *Dublin Independent*, and Nolin went to work as a machinist in a Dublin printing-office, and for a time also worked at Manchester, England, and other points, and then returned to Dublin. In November 1899 four men started from Dublin for America. They sailed from Liverpool, on a Red Star steamship of the American line, for Philadelphia. The steamer had a hard trip, and was given up for lost, but finally arrived in Philadelphia after nineteen days at sea. The four men from Dublin were four Johns, with Walsh the new one. Of the four men, Nolin and Walsh were reputed to be men of exceptional courage. Of Nolin it had been said, ' He would not fear to go aboard a boat with a belt of dynamite, and blow the boat to the bottom of the sea.' Of Walsh it was said, ' He feared not another man, even with a naked knife.' Walsh left behind him a wife and four children, living at No. 16, St. Michael's Hill, Dublin. He had worked the previous year as a horse tender for the Dublin Electric Tramway Company, W. M. H. Murphy being the superintendent. Nolin left a wife, but no children, in Castle

Street, Dublin. Merna left a wife at No. 88, Creaghton's Terrace, Dublin, and a sister, Mrs. Mary Tullman, at No. 31, Powers Street, Dublin. No charges of complicity in the explosions in Exchange Court, Dublin, had been made against any of the four men.

"The four Johns, after spending a few days in Philadelphia, in November 1899, went to New York. They stopped at the lodging- or boarding-house of John M. Kerr, at No. 45 Peck Slip, in the shipping district. They hung about New York until December 1899, when Rowan returned to Ireland, and went to work at his trade, he then being a fitter or first-class machinist in Dublin. In December 1899 Nolin and Walsh applied to the South Brooklyn branch of the Amalgamated Society of Machinists, an old English Society, with offshoots in America, and known in England as the Society of Engineers. Nolin and Walsh applied for donation money, which is $3 per week for those out of work. Nolin got donation money from John A. Shearman, secretary of the American Society of Machinists, who worked in the Pioneer Machine Works in Brooklyn, and to whom Nolin sent his card.

"In the last part of December 1899 Nolin, Walsh, and Merna went to Washington, D.C. Nolin remained there a short time, and then went on to Richmond, Virginia, where he went to work as a fitter in a foundry. On December 25th, 1899 (Christmas Day), Merna got a job in Washington as bar-tender at No. 212, Ninth Street, N.W., working for Joe McEnerney, a saloon-keeper. On January 1st, 1900, Walsh also got a job as bar-tender for McEnerney. Merna and Walsh relieved each other at the bar, and they shared a room together over the saloon. They worked as bar-tenders for McEnerney through January and February 1900 and along into March, while Nolin worked on in the Richmond foundry. Early in March Karl Dallman had registered at the Stafford House, in Buffalo, and then had gone away.

"On Monday evening, March 12th, Merna was found dead in his room over the saloon in Washington, where he and Walsh worked. He was found lying on the floor with a bullet in his heart. The marble slab of the bureau was torn

212

partly away. Beneath Merna was found a revolver, a 38-calibre British bulldog. Walsh was questioned, and he said Merna had entered the saloon in the evening in good spirits, laughed, chatted, went upstairs to their room, and fifteen minutes later he was found lying on the floor, dead. Suicide was the coroner's verdict, and Merna was buried in Washington on March 13th. Of the four Johns, two were left in America—Walsh in Washington and Nolin in Richmond.

"Somewhere about April 10th, 1900, Nolin received a communication from a lodge to which he belonged. The lodge was known in secret circles as the Napper Tandy Club. It was a Clan-na-Gael organisation. It mèt at Tom Moore's Hall, corner of Third Avenue and Sixteenth. Street, in New York. The entrance was at No. 149, East Sixteenth Street. Its president was a well-known bookseller. Nolin and Walsh both were members of this lodge. They were introduced by a man named Jack Hand, a sailor.

"Nolin's instructions, sent to him in Richmond, were for him to go to Washington, get John Walsh, and, with Walsh, go to Philadelphia, where, at a place specified as the Philadelphia and Reading Railroad Station, and a time fixed in the instructions at 7 p.m., on Saturday, April 14th, the two men, Nolin and Walsh, would meet a third man, who would give them further instructions as to what to do. Additional details, were arranged for. Nolin obeyed the instructions as they reached him. He left Richmond and went to Washington, where he got Walsh. When McEnerney heard Walsh was to leave he remonstrated and offered to raise Walsh's wages $12 per month if he would stay. Nolin and Walsh left Washington and went to the railroad station in Philadelphia specified in the instructions. That was on Saturday, April 14th, and about a quarter past seven in the evening, as they stood in the station, a well-dressed, stout man came up and asked if they were so-and-so. Nolin and Walsh replied satisfactorily, whereupon the stranger said : 'I am the man you want to see,' and the three men then had an earnest conversation, after which the stranger took $100 from his pocket and handed it to Nolin, along with two railroad tickets and two sleeping-car tickets from Philadelphia to Buffalo, over the Lehigh Valley Railroad. The stranger left the two men in the station, and Walsh and Nolin went to the Lehigh Valley train for Buffalo.

"Nolin and Walsh arrived in Buffalo at noon on Sunday, April 15th, over the Lehigh Valley Railroad. They went direct to the Stafford House and registered, as they had been told to register, as John Smith, of New York, and Thomas Moore, of Washington. They were assigned to room No. 88 and ordered up drinks. While waiting for the drinks there was a knock on the door. They said 'Come in.' The door opened and in stepped Dallman. He introduced himself and a satisfactory understanding of one another was reached. After dinner they took a walk in Buffalo together, going into a certain concert place, among others. They returned to the Stafford House, where Dallman was registered as Karl Dallman, Trenton, New Jersey. Dallman told Nolin and Walsh to prepare for an early start in the morning. After breakfast at the Stafford House on Monday morning, April 16th, Dallman gave to Nolin and Walsh two canvas grips or telescopes. In each of these grips were about eighty pounds of dynamite, mixed to about the consistency of stiff dough. It was in the form of a cake or loaf. Fuses were with each cake, lying on top, but not connected or attached. Dallman, Nolin, and Walsh left Buffalo together on Monday morning, April 16th, and took a trolley car to Niagara Falls, New York. On arriving at Niagara Falls Nolin and Walsh left Dallman and went to the Imperial Hotel, and registered there as Smith and Moore. In the afternoon Dallman called for them, and said: 'Now we will go across.' Dallman, Walsh, and Nolin took a Grand Trunk train across Suspension Bridge and got off at Merriton, in Canada, and took a street-car at Merriton, and then went to Thorold, where Mrs. Constable saw them near the lock. When Nolin and Walsh and Dallman returned to the Falls that night, Nolin and Walsh, at Dallman's request, arranged to change their lodgings, and the next day, Tuesday, April 17th, they left the Imperial Hotel and went to the

214

Dolphin House. Dallman went to the Rosli House on the Canada side of the Falls. Dallman, Nolin, and Walsh went driving together, and on Thursday afternoon, April 19th, Nolin and Walsh drove to Thorold, meeting Dallman, also driving, on the road near Thorold. The cabman and the liveryman's hired man, who drove Dallman, Identified the the three men. The three met on the American side, Dallman calling on them at the Dolphin House and they crossing and seeing Dallman.

"Walsh took the dynamite into Canada. He went from the Dolphin House to the Rosli House. At a quarter past three on Friday afternoon, April 20th, he carried one of the bags of dynamite over, and at one o'clock on Saturday afternoon, April 21st, the day of the explosion, he carried the other bag over. The first bag was left with Dallman over-night, and the second bag was taken over and left with it on Saturday afternoon until Nolin and Walsh started for Thorold. Dallman gave Nolin and Walsh money for hotel bills and incidental expenses. After the explosion they were to meet at the Falls, or failing there, meet in Buffalo and take late trains away. The explosion, the arrests, the convictions, and the sentence for life followed.

"Karl Dallman clearly was the most interesting figure in the entire affair. I sent his picture and his description to trusted friends in various cities and in due time I learned that Karl Dallman of Trenton, New Jersey, was none other than Luke Dillon, of Philadelphia, Pennsylvania. At one time he was a member of the executive of the Clan-na-Gael, and defended it and publicly championed its cause, and achieved more than national prominence when, as a member of the executive committee of the Clan-na-Gael, he went to Chicago, at the time of the murder of Dr. Cronin, and denounced Alexander Sullivan, raised funds for the prosecution of those accused of murdering Dr. Cronin ; advocated the throwing off of the oath of secrecy, so far as necessary to run down Cronin's assassins ; went on the witness stand and, by his testimony, revealed the secret of the Triangle, the chief three who had ruled as the executive of the Clan-na-Gael ; made public the charges against Sullivan and fought throughout on the side of the anti-Sullivan wing.   The identification was made absolute and final.   Men who knew Luke Dillon, who had worked day by day near him, went to see Karl Dallman and identified him positively as Luke Dillon.   But more than all that, the Government knows that Karl Dallman is Luke Dillon as certainly and as surely as it knows that I am John W. Murray.

"Dillon was a shoemaker originally. In 1881 he was shoemaking at No. 639, Paul Street, Philadelphia. He was married and for five years he lived in Paul Street, making a speciality of slipper-making, and in 1884 he added a small stock of shoes, becoming a shoedealer as well as a shoemaker. In 1887 he moved into a little brick house at No. 920, Passyunk Avenue. He became active and prominent in the Clan-na-Gael. When a split came he espoused the side of the Cronin faction, known as the United Brotherhood, which later merged into the Irish Revolutionary Brotherhood. Dr. Cronin formerly lived at St. Catharine's, near Thorold, where the explosion occurred. In May 1889 he was murdered in Chicago. About 1891 Dillon abandoned the shoe business, and 1892 found him a teller in the Dime Savings Bank at No. 1429, Chestnut Street, Philadelphia. In 1899 he moved, with his family, to Federal Street, Philadelphia, where he was living in 1900, when he went to Thorold. The bank went into other hands eventually, turning over its deposits and accounts to the Union Surety Guarantee Company, across the street. In March and April he made trips to Buffalo, and on April 10th, the day Nolin received the communication to go to Washington and get Walsh, Dillon started for Buffalo, registered as Dallman at the Stafford House the next day, and the day after, on April 12th, went to Canada, in the vicinity of Thorold, and was registered at the Rosli House on the Canada side, where later he stopped, while Walsh and Nolin were at the Dolphin House. This was two days before Walsh and Nolin left Philadelphia. Dillon returned to the United States, and on April 14th again was at the Stafford House to meet Walsh and Nolin, who left Philadelphia that night and arrived the next afternoon. On the following Saturday, after the three men had been together all the week, the explosion occurred.

"For two years after the three men went to Kingston for life the general public knew nothing of the identity of Karl Dallman. Then the *Buffalo Express* made known the fact, telling the story of his life and connection with the Cronin affair. Some of Dillon's friends explained that he had gone to South Africa to fight with the Boers against the British, and may have been killed there. The truth is that Luke Dillon is in Kingston Penitentiary. He went there as Karl Dallman. From the moment of his entrance he lost all names, real or assumed, and is known only by a number. Inmates are numbered, not named, in Kingston. He is a silent figure, grey-haired, white-faced, prison-garbed. He works during the day and when night comes, he lets down his shelf or bed of iron from the wall, blankets it and lies down to read. The light overhead goes out. The velvet purr of a cushioned tread hovers a moment by his door and dies away. Then all is still—and the stillness of the night in Kingston is a silence as grim as the great grey walls that shut out the world."

39

THE TEMPORARY QUIRK MYSTERY

AFTER his long search for all the essential details of the past lives of the three dynamitards, Murray returned to find a series of systematic attempts being made to derail trains on the Canadian Pacific Railroad's lines beyond Fort William. The favourite place for these attempts was about seventy miles west of Fort William. He went to the vicinity, and after patient work and waiting enmeshed one of the ringleaders, who was convicted, and sent to prison, and the gang was broken up. It was July 1901 when he finally landed his man. In the following session of Parliament an Act was passed investing him with the full powers of a coroner throughout the entire province, with authority to hold inquests and conduct official inquiries into the causes of fires. This investiture occurred on February 8th, 1902. Less than a month thereafter another murder mystery arose.

" In the city of Brantford lived James Quirk and John Toole," says Murray. " Quirk was a famed sport and sprinter, and sharper. They kept an hotel called the Commercial House in Brantford. Quirk was insured for about $14,000 on his life. He was married, and had two young daughters. The rooms of Quirk, Mrs. Quirk, the daughters and Toole were along the same hall. In fact Mrs. Quirk's room opened into her daughters' room, and her daughters' room opened into Toole's room.

" On Sunday, March 6th, 1902, Quirk went out for the evening. About eleven o'clock that night he returned to the hotel. Toole was in the office as was a cook at the hotel named Ryan, who had been out with some friends that evening, and had returned ahead of Quirk, and was somewhat under the influence of liquor. Evidence given later at the inquest showed that Quirk went out toward the bar in the rear. Toole shortly after followed Quirk out toward the bar, telling a bell-boy named Eddie Kennedy, who was on duty, that he could go to bed. Kennedy went upstairs, leaving Ryan in the office, and Quirk and Toole somewhere back in the rear. A minute or two later, George Rillis, a bar-tender of the Kirby House, walked in, and asked for Quirk.

" 'He just stepped into the bar,' said Ryan. Rillis walked out to the cubby-hole, where they passed out drinks from the bar to the front. He knocked and called. There was no response. Rillis walked back to the office.

" 'Quirk is not there,' he said.

" 'He may have stepped out,' said Ryan.

" The bell-boy, Eddie Kennedy, ran downstairs into the office.

" 'Something's wrong in the stable!' he said excitedly. ' I heard a noise of groaning from my room.'

" Ryan and Rillis rose and went out into the stable, going to the harness-room. They found Quirk lying in a pool of blood, gasping his last breath. He was unable to speak. Ryan ran into the house, and upstairs and rapped at Toole's door. There was no response. Ryan then knocked on Mrs. Quirk's door. The rooms of Toole and Mrs. Quirk opened into the room of Mrs. Quirk's daughters, which was between. Ryan also roused the people in the house. Mrs. Quirk came out of her room.

" 'Jim is killed,' she was told.

" At first it was thought she really had fainted. Mrs. Quirk later said that she went into Toole's room, and he was sitting in a chair reading a paper, and he jumped up, and came through the daughters' room, and out of her room, and went out to the stable. When Toole was seen by others later he was bloody, and this was explained by the statement that when he entered the stable and saw Quirk lying dead he grabbed him by the head and was spattered with blood.

" The theory advanced was that Quirk had been climbing to the loft to look at some game chickens he kept there, and that he missed his footing, and fell head foremost to the floor, where he lay moaning until Kennedy, the bell-boy heard him. This theory is not tenable. The blood spatters showed a murder, and not an accidental fall. Quirk was struck with an iron bar, or an axe with a blunt head, or a weapon of that kind. It was a murder, not an accident.

"The coroner's inquest was prolonged by many postponements for months. No licence for an hotel bar was granted to Mrs. Quirk or to Toole. The insurance companies refused to pay the policies, amounting to $14,000, on Quirk's life.

"Mrs. Quirk and Toole left Brantford, and sojourned for a time in Buffalo, New York.

"The case is a mystery that is a mystery only in so far as the formal legal solution of it is concerned. I am in hopes of getting at the bottom of the case eventually, as I am morally certain who the guilty parties are, but there is not sufficient evidence just yet to convict, in case they are arrested. In such cases the desired links in the chain of evidence sometimes come quite quickly and very unexpectedly. At other times they come deliberately and after some delay. But this case is one where all the subsequent circumstances tend to indicate that it may be just a matter of delay until what we are waiting for comes to pass. When it does there will be an arrest, and when there is an arrest I believe certainly there will be a conviction.

"I do not think Jimmy Quirk's murderer sleeps any too soundly at night during these days of anxious freedom. In fact I think the murderer is beginning to realise that in the end the full proof of guilt is doomed to come out. The murderer knows the very evidence desired, and it simply is a question of time, when some occurrence may leave the murderer without ability to withhold it any longer."

40

TWO CROOKS IN CLOVER

AN interruption to the work of drawing out evidence at the Jimmy Quirk inquest in Brantford occurred in July 1902, when Murray obtained a trace of the whereabouts of two crooks who had lived on the fat of the land in the counties of Kent and Essex and Elgin the year before, and had skipped out to no one knew where, when the farmers rose up and determined to put an end to their depredations.

"They were a pair of gay buckos," says Murray. "They stole right and left. Various daring burglaries were committed in the counties of Kent, Essex, and Elgin. They were not slovenly, ordinary jobs, but were robberies cunningly planned and skilfully executed. They operated in city and country alike, plundering farmhouses and barns, and looting safes and stores. They made some good hauls of jewellery and money in the city of Chatham. The jobs were not the work of novices or of timid crooks. The thieves were men willing to take a chance and run a long risk.

"The farmers were up in arms, and arranged for a systematic watch for the burglars. In due time they were rewarded, for the robbers were discovered in the act of stealing fifty bushels of clover seed. The thieves had a team, and away they went with the stolen clover seeds, and with the farmers in pursuit. Over the roads they sped pell-mell, lickety-split. One of the thieves was a man past middle age. He scooted on ahead with the booty, while the farmers gave chase to the other crook, and after a mile or more of fast going they got him. He was winded, and they handed him over to a constable in Ridgetown. No sooner did he regain his wind and get his bearings than he gave the constable the slip and was off like a flash. Pursuit was futile this time, for he was beyond reach, and had disappeared before the chase could be organised.

" The trail of the older crook, however, led to a house and barn near Ridgetown. When searchers arrived there the pair of thieves had skipped. A hunt for plunder failed to reveal any trace of the whereabouts of the clover seed. It was neither in nor under the house or barn. There was no sign of its having been buried, and it was not secreted in a chimney or in bags tied in the trees. Some birds were noticed flying in and flying out of an opening to an old well. This opening was investigated, and the clover seed was found dumped in the old well. Clover seed was worth over $8 a bushel at that time, and the abandoned well had about $500 worth of seed in it.

" From descriptions and other details, it was easy to identify the two crooks as Ben Reilly and John Acker. Reilly was thirty-eight years old, and had lived at Ridgetown, renting the house and barn. Acker was fifty years old. I billed them throughout Canada and the United States. In due time we heard of them, one in Ohio and the other in Indiana. They had separated. I prepared the necessary extradition papers, and went to Fort Wayne, Indiana, and with the assistance of Detective Mahoney in Windsor, arrested Reilly in Conway, Ohio, and Acker in Bluffton, Indiana. When they came before the United States Commissioner, in July 1902, their defence against extradition was an alibi. I had three respectable and responsible witnesses who identified them positively. One of the witnesses was Liveryman Jones, from whom they had hired a team. Another of the witnesses was Blacksmith David Olone, and the third was Constable Mills.

" The Gaynor and Green cases had been prominent in Quebec about this time. Gaynor and Green were fugitives from the United States, and were living in Quebec. The United States failed in its efforts to extradite them. Officials in the United States felt they had not been treated fairly in the Gaynor and Green matter, and I do not think they were. When the evidence in the case of Acker and Reilly was all in, the United States Commissioner held it under consideration, and finally dismissed the prisoners.

"The case clearly was in violation of extradition law. An alibi is for a jury to hear. All that is necessary in either country under the extradition law is to have the prisoners identified. However, a Canada official was not in a position to take any lofty attitude on an extradition case just at that time, for Gaynor and Green were enjoying life in Quebec, and they were fugitives of far more public importance than Acker and Reilly. They were accused of matters involving hundreds of thousands of dollars, which was quite different from a few burglaries and fifty bushels of clover seed hid in an old well.

"One of Acker's friends met me as I was leaving the Commissioner's office.

"'I think John ought to write a note to Gaynor thanking him for his forethought,' he said. Then he added, confidentially, 'You know Acker and Gaynor are first-namers alike, both being John, and their ain't so much difference in their ages. One John stays in the States and the other John stays in Canada. I hope the two countries never exchange Johns.'"